Spelling Success

CLASS 1

Peter Clutterbuck

Blake
EDUCATION
Better ways to learn

To Jessie O'Brien

Spelling Success Class 1

Published by Scholastic India Pvt. Ltd.
A-27, Ground Floor, Sigma Centre
Infocity-1, Sector 34, Gurgaon-122001 (India)
Info-in@scholastic.asia

Author: Peter Clutterbuck
Editor: Kerry Davies
Cover and internal design: Janice Bowles
Typesetter: Julian Mole, Post Pre Press.

ISBN: 978-93-5471-953-0
First edition 2010
This reprint edition: June, 2025
Printed in India

Contents

Contents continued

Term 3

Term 4

About This Book

The *Spelling Success* series provides students with learning activities that embrace the different elements of the spelling system. Each book focuses on the different scope and sequences in the development of spelling skills for each age group or skill level.

Book 1 provides students with user-friendly activities to master and develop spelling skills for this vital year of education. It is during this year that students first experience the complexities of the way we form words using letters in a correct sequence. They develop strategies for using sounds and visual patterns to help them strengthen and reinforce their knowledge, building up a comprehensive supply of ready words for written work.

The activities in each book are sequential through the four terms of the school year. This means that it's best to start at the beginning of the Term 1 section and work though to the end, before commencing Term 2 activities, and so on. There are 76 units in this book, 18 per term plus four Review and Test units. Each term is divided into the four areas of knowledge that need to be understood and learned in order to develop a comprehensive mastery of spelling:

Phonological Knowledge — how words sound

Word Function Knowledge — how word function can change spelling

Meaning Knowledge — how context can change word form

Word Fun — puzzles to excite interest in words and spelling

The Phonological Knowledge and the Word Function Knowledge sections include Revision and Test sheets for each term. Four units of Review and Test sheets covering the whole book are provided at the end of Term 4.

This book also contains useful tools to support students with their spelling. At the back of the book you'll find:

- ★ Useful Words list
- ★ WINK: Words I Need to Know — space to record problematic words
- ★ Some Tips for Learning to Spell
- ★ Assessment checklist
- ★ Glossary of Terms

Answers to all activities are provided in a special liftout section. A useful **topic list** for the whole year is given before the units.

Spelling Success provides an integrated method of teaching phonics, spelling and vocabulary. These books will improve literacy skills through effective instruction and evaluation based on the latest research into how spelling is best taught and learned successfully.

Book 1 Topic Chart

TOPIC	UNIT
Adding final letters	49
Adding initial letters	48
Adding vowels	46,47
Anagrams	52,53
Bigger or smaller?	18
Compound words	34,35
Consonant blends	60
Find the words	54,72
Homophones	16,17
Jumbled letters	71
Letter patterns	28,29,30,31
More than one, adding **s**	12,13
r-Influenced vowels, **ar**	55
r-Influenced vowels, **or**	56
Reading and drawing	70
Short and long words	11
Short **a** sound	19
Short **e** sound	20
Short **i** sound	21
Short **o** sound	22
Short **u** sound	23
Sound patterns, **ai**	58
Sound patterns, **ay** and **oy**	37

TOPIC	UNIT
Sound patterns, **ch**	41
Sound patterns, **ck**	40
Sound patterns, **ee**	59
Sound patterns, long and short **oo**	42
Sound patterns, **oa**	57
Sound patterns, final **sh**	39
Sound patterns, initial **sh**	38
Sounds and symbols, **b** and **g**	1
Sounds and symbols, **d** and **c**	3
Sounds and symbols, **h** and **f**	2
Sounds and symbols, **j** and **l**	4
Sounds and symbols, **m** and **n**	5
Sounds and symbols, **p** and **r**	6
The alphabet	10
Word building, adding letters	65
Word building, changing letters	64
Word building, initial letters	66
Word building, word sums	67
Word endings, **all** and **y**	24
Writing in code	36

Sounds and symbols, b and g

UNIT 1

Look at the pictures.
Put a cross (×) in the box for those that begin with b.
Put a tick (✓) in the box for those that begin with g.

1.

2.

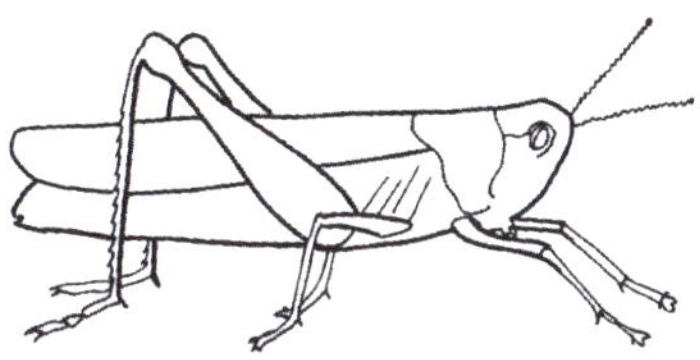

3.

4.

5.

6.

Parent/Teacher Signature Date

UNIT 2

Sounds and symbols, f and h

Look at the pictures.
Put a cross (×) in the box for those that begin with f.
Put a tick (✓) in the box for those that begin with h.

1. 	2. 	3. 
4. 	5. 	6. 

Parent/Teacher Signature Date

Sounds and symbols, c and d

Look at the pictures.
Put a cross (×) in the box for those that begin with c.
Put a tick (✓) in the box for those that begin with d.

1.	2.	3.

4.	**5.**	**6.**
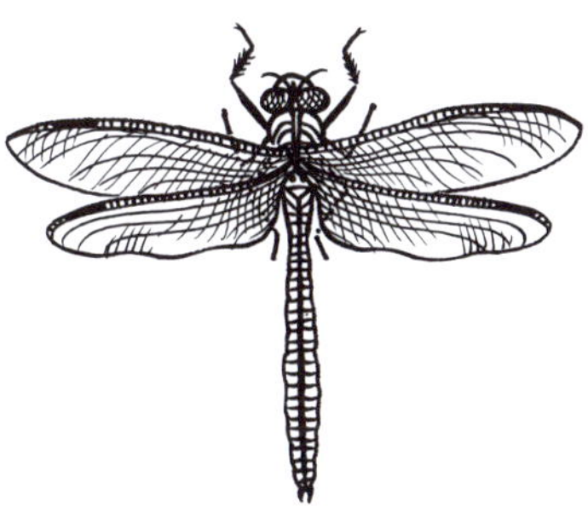		

Parent/Teacher Signature Date

UNIT 4

Sounds and symbols, j and l

Look at the pictures.
Put a cross (×) in the box for those that begin with j.
Put a tick (✓) in the box for those that begin with l.

1. 	2. 	3. 
4. 	5. 	6. 

Parent/Teacher Signature Date

Sounds and symbols, m and n

Look at the pictures.
Put a cross (×) in the box for those that begin with m.
Put a tick (✓) in the box for those that begin with n.

1.

2.

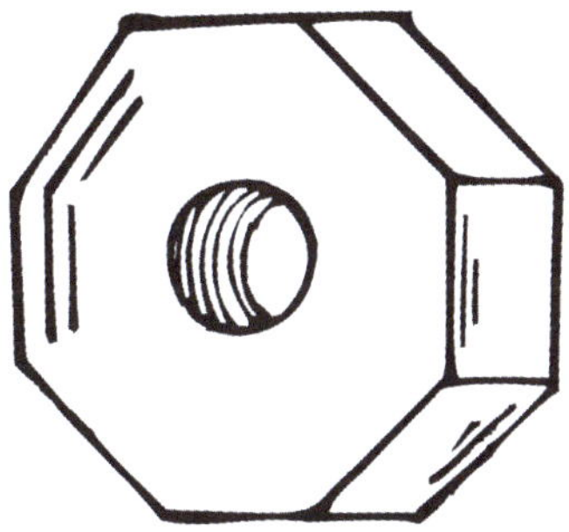

3.

4.

5.

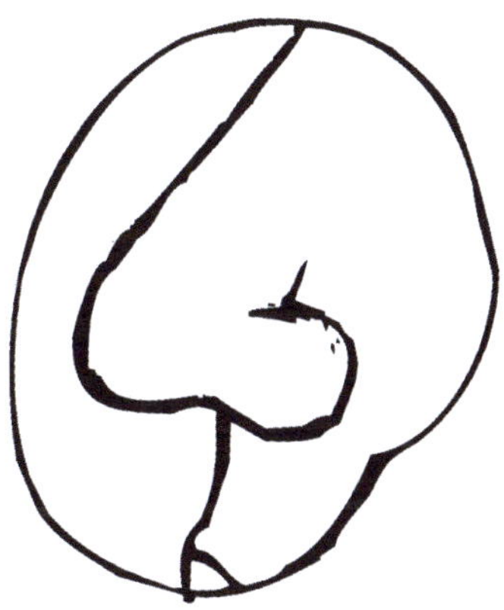

6.

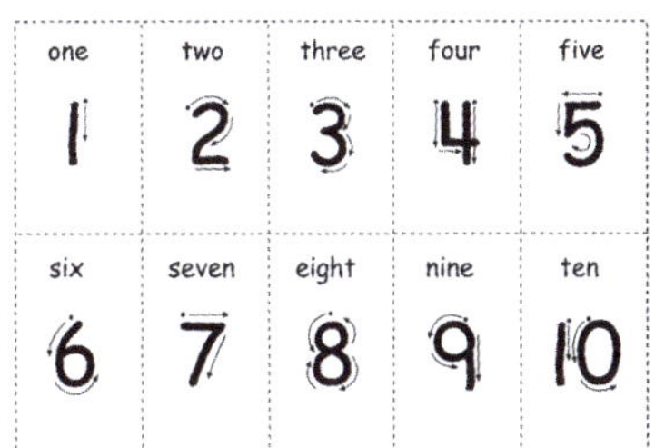

Parent/Teacher Signature Date

UNIT 6

Sounds and symbols, p and r

Look at the pictures.
Put a cross (×) in the box for those that begin with **p**.
Put a tick (✓) in the box for those that begin with **r**.

1. 	**2.** 	**3.** 
4. 	**5.** 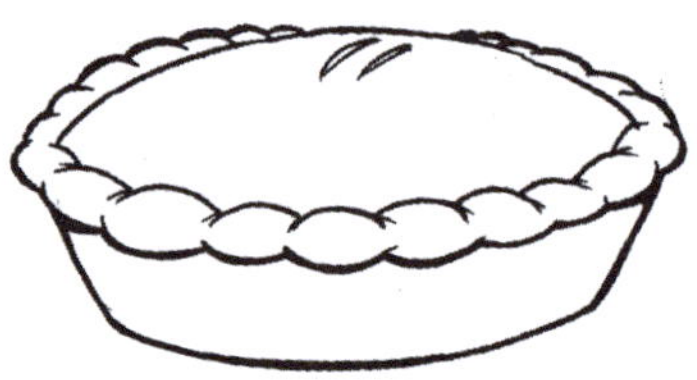	**6.** 

Parent/Teacher Signature Date

Revision

Fill in the space in the boxes with the letter that begins each word.

n **d** **h** **g** **j** **b**

1.

_____one

2.

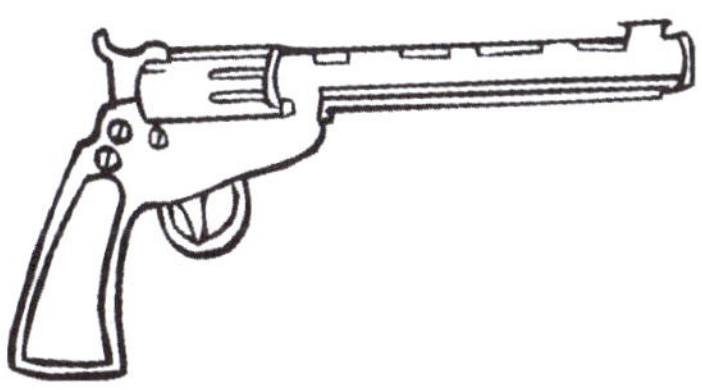

______un

3.

_____at

4.

_____ug

5.

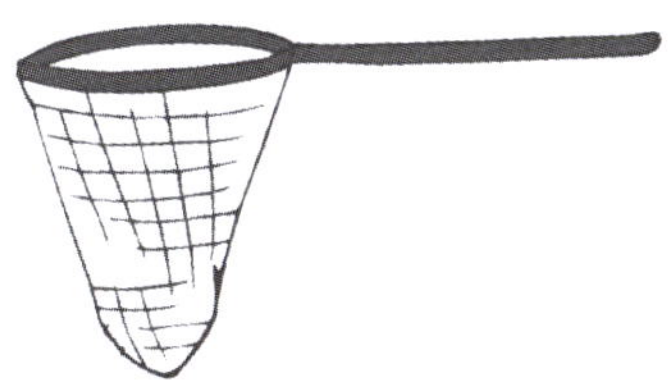

_____et

6.

_____uck

Parent/Teacher Signature Date

Test 1

The underlined word is spelled wrongly because it begins with the wrong letter. Write the word correctly in the space.

1 I read a <u>sook</u>. [1]

2 I go to <u>ted</u> at 9 o'clock. [2]

3 The <u>mox</u> chased the chickens. [3]

4 Our <u>pat</u> had three kittens. [4]

5 I filled the <u>bug</u> with water. [5]

6 The number after eight is <u>pine</u>. [6]

Total correct ______ / 6

Parent/Teacher Signature Date

Test 2

Choose the correct word from the brackets. Write it in the space.

1 I ate a (pie, tie). 1

2 In summer Tom wears a (tat, hat). 2

3 Ella's (mog, dog) likes bones. 3

4 My parents drive a blue (car, far). 4

5 She climbed up the (ladder, padder). 5

6 The number after four is (hive, five). 6

Total correct ______ / 6

Parent/Teacher Signature Date

UNIT 10

The alphabet

Look at the letters of the alphabet.

a	b	c	d	e	f	g	h
i	j	k	l	m	n	o	p
q	r	s	t	u	v	w	x
y	z						

1. Which letter comes after **e**? ________
2. Which letter comes after **h**? ________
3. Which letter comes after **g**? ________
4. Which letter comes before **k**? ________
5. Which letter comes before **b**? ________
6. Which letter comes between **r** and **t**? ________
7. Which letter comes between **f** and **h**? ________
8. Which two letters have dots on top? ________ and ________

Parent/Teacher Signature Date

Short and long words

We use letters to make words.
Some words we make are short, such as:
in to a dog cat

Some words are long, such as:
butter elephant bananas window giraffe

Look at the words in the box below.

us	**mother**	**asleep**	**rat**	**of**
on	**apple**	**played**	**is**	**winter**
I	**football**	**automobile**	**the**	**it**
log	**computer**	**buckets**	**off**	**history**

Put the words from the box into these two lists.

Short words	**Long words**
________________	________________
________________	________________
________________	________________
________________	________________
________________	________________
________________	________________
________________	________________
________________	________________
________________	________________
________________	________________

Parent/Teacher Signature Date

UNIT 12

More than one, adding s 1

We can add **s** to make a word mean more than one. For example, you can have one **apple**, but two **apples**.

Make the second word mean more than one and write it on the line. The first one has been done for you.

 **1.** one pig two *pigs*	 **6.** one hat two ____________
 **2.** one tree three ____________	 **7.** one ball four ____________
 **3.** one star three ____________	 **8.** one bird two ____________
 **4.** one book four ____________	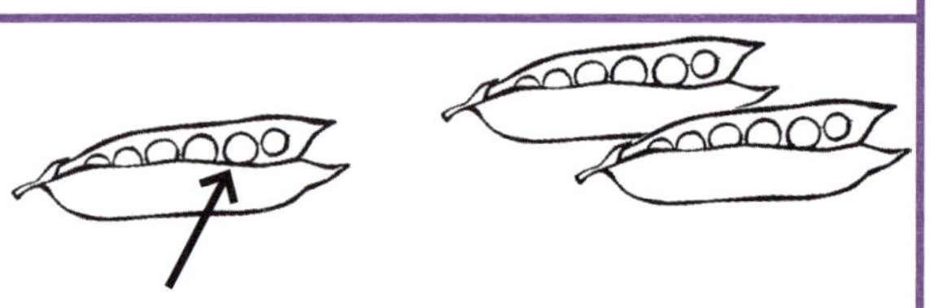 **9.** one pea lots of ____________
 **5.** one clock two ____________	 **10.** one ant three ____________

Parent/Teacher Signature Date

More than one, adding s 2

We can add **s** to make a word mean more than one.

A Make the second word mean more than one and write it on the line.

1. one toy two ____________

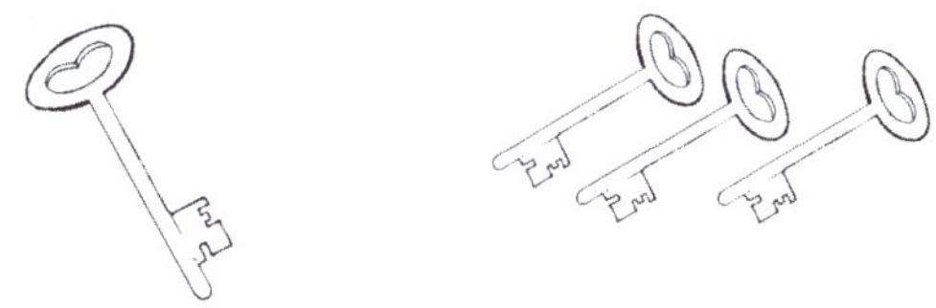

4. one key three ____________

2. one shop two ____________

5. one hen three ____________

3. one flower two ____________

6. one chair four ____________

B Now make each word in brackets mean more than one and write it on the line.

1. A lot of ____________ ate the cheese. (rat)
2. There are four ____________ in the room. (bed)
3. A bird laid six ____________. (egg)
4. The farmer has twenty ____________. (cow)

Parent/Teacher Signature Date

UNIT 14

Revision

Look at the words in the box below. Rewrite each word under the correct heading below.

toys	flower	girl
day	bone	pig
girls	toy	days
pigs	bones	flowers

One	More than one
______	______
______	______
______	______
______	______
______	______
______	______

Parent/Teacher Signature Date

Test

Choose the correct word in the brackets and write it in the space.

1 There are two (dog, dogs). [1]

2 I saw six (cows, cow). [2]

3 We picked one (flowers, flower). [3]

4 The dog ate a (bones, bone). [4]

5 Riley has lots of (toy, toys). [5]

6 Our classroom has six (chair, chairs). [6]

Total correct ______
6

Parent/Teacher Signature Date

UNIT 16

Homophones 1

Homophones are words that sound the same but have different spellings and different meanings.

Write the correct word under the pictures.

1. son, sun

____

2. sea, see

____

3. tale, tail

____

4. four, for

4

____

5. to, two

2

____

6. one, won

____

Parent/Teacher Signature Date

Homophones 2

UNIT 17

Homophones are words that sound the same but have different spellings and different meanings.

Circle the correct word to complete each sentence.

1.

Emily (won, one) the race.

2.

This boat has a striped (sail, sale).

3.

The prisoner was kept in a (sell, cell).

4.

I am going to (sell, cell) my iPod.

5.

There is only (won, one) lolly left.

6.

We went to the (sail, sale) at the supermarket.

Parent/Teacher Signature Date

UNIT 18

Bigger or smaller?

A Circle only the words that name things that are bigger than a dog.

cup	house	book
boat	ant	rat
bee	pin	man
train	tree	grub

B Now circle only the words that name things that are smaller than a chair.

rabbit	fly	flower
bulldozer	elephant	school
giraffe	bee	grasshopper
mouse	bus	ball

Parent/Teacher Signature Date

UNIT 19

Short a sound

The letter **a** is often sounded as a short sound, as in the words **dad** and **sad**.

A Add the letter **a** to complete each word that matches the picture. Say each word aloud.

1. 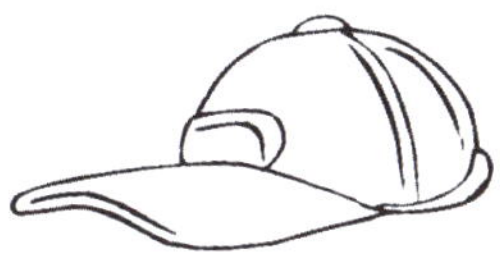 c_____p	**4.**  h_____t
2. 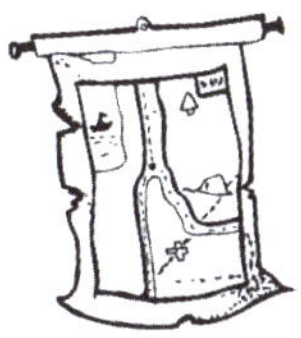 m_____p	**5.** 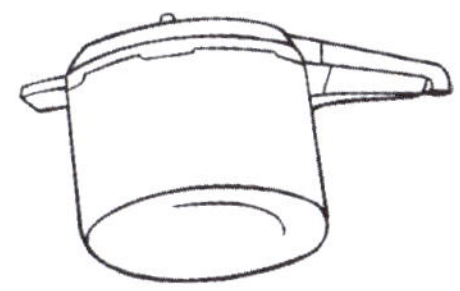 p_____n
3. 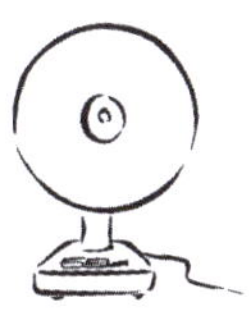 f_____n	**6.**  t_____p

B Circle the word that is the same as the one at the top.

1. bad	**2. sat**	**3. pan**	**4. fat**
bed	sit	pan	fit
bid	sat	pin	fun
box	set	pat	fox
bad	sun	pet	fat

Parent/Teacher Signature Date

Short e sound

The letter **e** often makes a short sound, as in **men** and **met**.

A Add the letter **e** in the space to complete each word that matches the picture. Say each word aloud.

1.  b_____d	**2.** 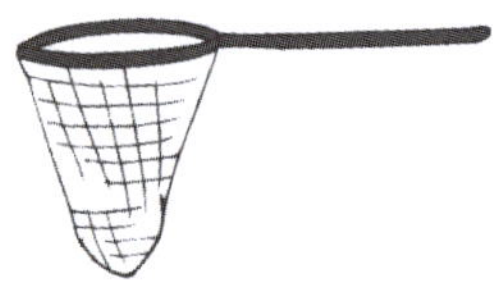 n_____t	**3.**  t_____n
4.  h_____n	**5.** 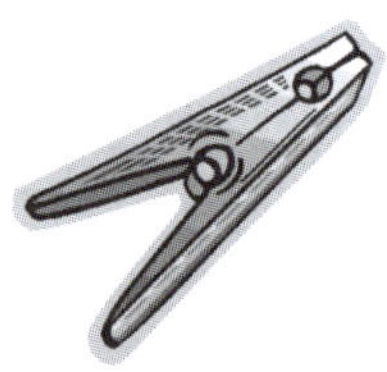 p_____g	**6.**  l_____g

B Circle the words in each row that sound the same.

1.	men	nut	ten	bit
2.	leg	net	tin	jet
3.	tap	get	lip	met
4.	pen	gun	hen	mat

Parent/Teacher Signature Date

Short i sound

The letter i can make a short sound, as in the words **rib** and **dig**.

A Add the letter i in the space to complete each word that matches the picture. Say each word aloud.

1. 6 s____x	**2.**  p____n	**3.**  p____g
4. 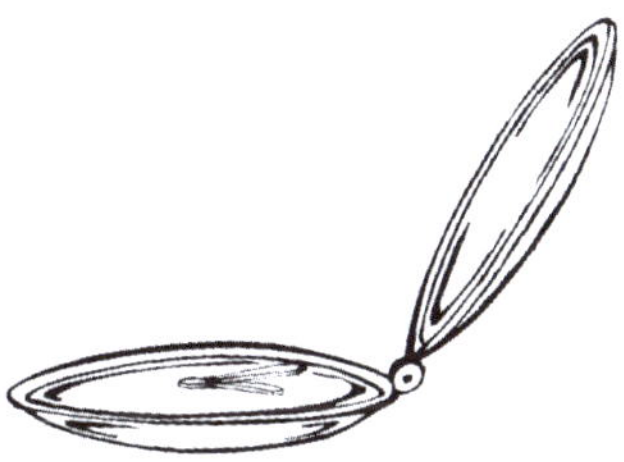 l____d	**5.**  f____n	**6.**  b____n

B Add the letters at the top to the letter below to make each word and write it on the line.

it	ip
1. b ________	**4.** s ________
2. f ________	**5.** l ________
3. l ________	**6.** h ________

Parent/Teacher Signature Date

UNIT 22

Short o sound

The letter **o** can make a short sound, as in **bob** and **rob**.

A Add the letter **o** in the space to make a word that matches the picture. Say each word aloud.

1. 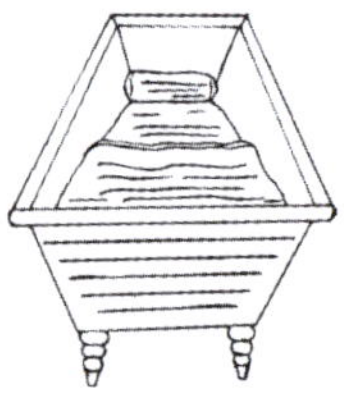 c_____t	**2.**  m_____p	**3.**  f_____x
4.  d_____g	**5.** 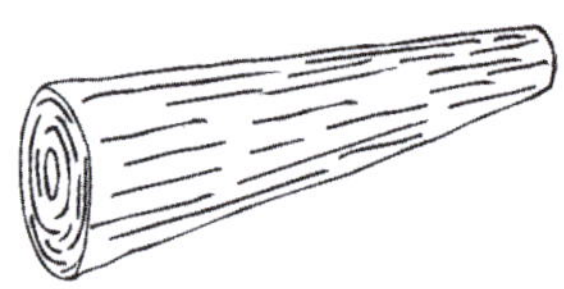 l_____g	**6.**  b_____x

B The words in the box have been cramped up. Find each short word and write it in the space.

tophotpothopfoggot

1. I __________ a bike for my birthday.
2. We climbed all the way to the __________ of the hill.
3. We cooked the meat in the __________.
4. Today it is cold but yesterday it was __________.
5. We could not see in the thick __________.
6. A frog can __________.

Parent/Teacher Signature Date

Short **u** sound

The letter **u** often makes a short sound, like the words **run** and **tub**.

A Add the letter **u** in the space to make a word that matches the picture. Say each word aloud.

1.	**2.**	**3.**
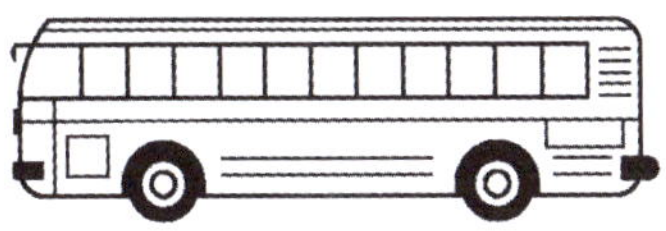 b_____s	 s_____n	 c_____p
4.  t_____g	**5.**  j_____g	**6.**  h_____t

B The words in the box have been cramped up. Find each short word and write it on the lines below. Then draw a picture.

rugpupsuntub

1. ____________________	2. ____________________
3. ____________________	4. ____________________

Parent/Teacher Signature Date

Word endings, all and y

A Many words end in the letters **all** and are sounded as in the words **call** and **stall**.

Write **all** in the space to make a word that matches the picture.

1.  h_______	**2.**  b_______	**3.** 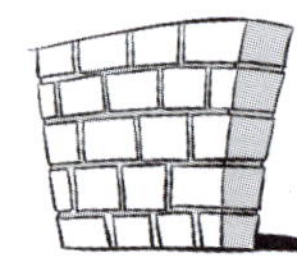 w_______
4.  sm_______	**5.**  f_______	**6.**  t_______

B Many words end in the letter **y** and make a long **i** sound, as in the words **why** and **buy**.

Write each word from the box in its correct sentence below.

my	cry	dry	fly	sky	try

1. You must always ___________ hard.
2. Today it is wet but yesterday it was ___________.
3. We could see the sun in the ___________.
4. When he lost his ice-cream the boy began to ___________.
5. That is ___________ seat over there.
6. A bird can ___________.

Parent/Teacher Signature   Date

Revision

A Look at the pictures. Put a cross (×) in the box for those that sound like **pat** and put a tick (✓) in the box for those that sound like **hug**.

1. 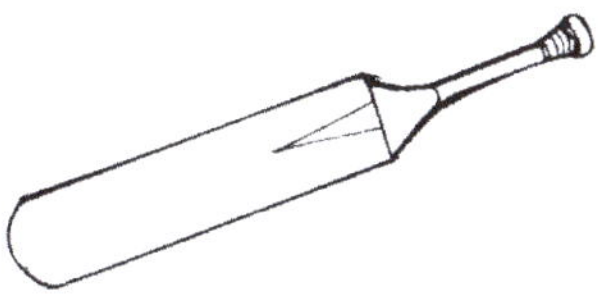	**2.** 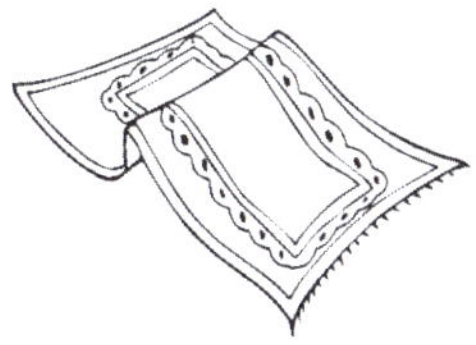	**3.** 
4. 	**5.** 	**6.** 

B Look at the pictures. Put a cross (×) in the box for those that sound like **den** and put a tick (✓) in the box for those that sound like **tin**.

1. 	**2.** 	**3.** 
4. 	**5.** 	**6.** 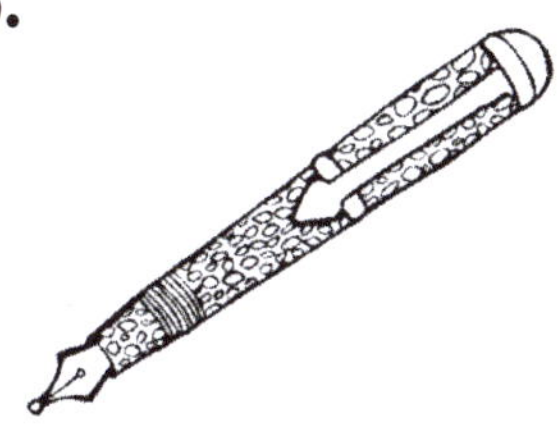

Parent/Teacher Signature Date

UNIT 26

Test 1

Choose the correct word from the brackets and write it in the space.

1 I wore a (hat, pan) on my head. [1]

2 A (hit, hen) lays eggs. [2]

3 We put the rubbish in the (bin, ban). [3]

4 A baby sleeps in a (cat, cot). [4]

5 I ate a (bun, bin) for lunch. [5]

6 A (ball, bell) can bounce. [6]

Total correct ______ / 6

Parent/Teacher Signature   Date

Test 2

Add the correct letter from the brackets to complete each word. Write the word in the space.

1 We cooked the eggs in a p___n. (i, a) [1]

2 The fish were caught in the n___t. (a, e) [2]

3 The number after five is s___x. (i, u) [3]

4 My c___t (u, a) likes to chase mice. [4]

5 You can put water in a j___g. (a, u) [5]

6 We climbed over the brick w___ll. (a, u) [6]

Total correct ____ / 6

Parent/Teacher Signature Date

UNIT 28

Letter patterns 1

Draw a line from the word to its picture.

1. date
   plate
   gate

2. snail
   mail
   tail

3. dish
   fish
   wish

4. bake
   cake
   take

5. mice
   rice
   lice

6. give
   live
   five

8. flask
   task
   mask

8. lock
   rock
   clock

9. seed
   weed
   feed

Parent/Teacher Signature   Date

Letter patterns 2

Look at the words in the boxes below. Write each word under the letter patterns they contain below.

 gate	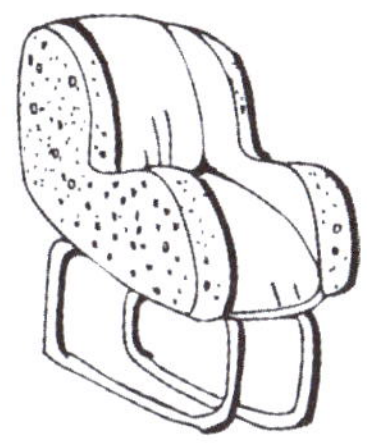 seat	 mice
 wheat	 dice	 plate

ice	eat	ate
______________	______________	______________
______________	______________	______________

Parent/Teacher Signature Date

UNIT 30

Letter patterns 3

A From the groups of words below, find and write the word that does **not** contain the same letter pattern.

1. sky, find, kind ______________
2. dust, live, must ______________
3. hair, table, fair ______________
4. bone, zone, baby ______________
5. gold, book, fold ______________
6. bell, fell, wish ______________

B Write each word in the box under its letter pattern below.

face	**bone**	**dear**	**done**	**gone**
bear	**race**	**fear**	**lace**	

ear	ace	one
______________	______________	______________
______________	______________	______________
______________	______________	______________

Parent/Teacher Signature Date

Letter patterns 4

A Add a letter pattern from the box to complete each word below to match the picture.

ite **oot** **uck** **ar** **est** **ell**

1.  b________	**2.** 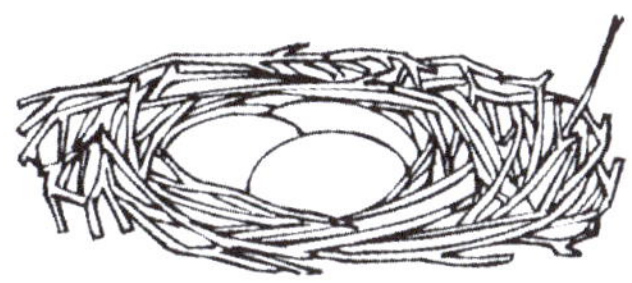 n________	**3.**  st________
4.  d________	**5.**  b________	**6.** 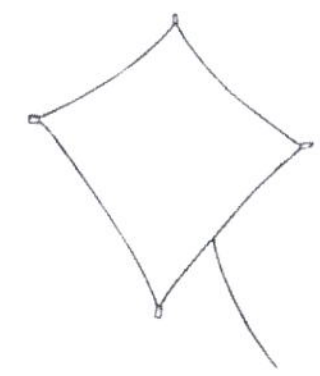 k________

B Circle the word that matches the picture.

1. work
   pork
   fork

2. road
   load
   toad

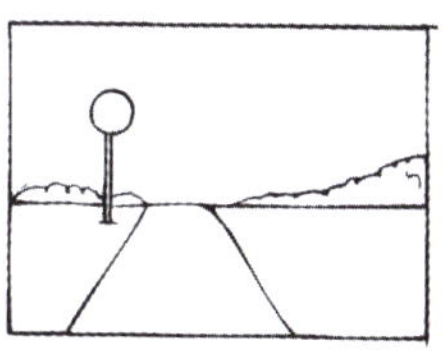

3. hook
   book
   took

Parent/Teacher Signature Date

UNIT 32

Revision

A Circle the word that does not contain the same letter pattern.

1.	mill	will	fill	bird	till
2.	steer	beer	queer	deer	four
3.	hill	screw	drew	crew	flew
4.	ball	sale	call	hall	wall
5.	gold	old	fall	fold	cold

B Add the correct letter pattern to match the picture.

1. (one, old)

b________

2. (oot, orn)

f________

3. (ate, ite)

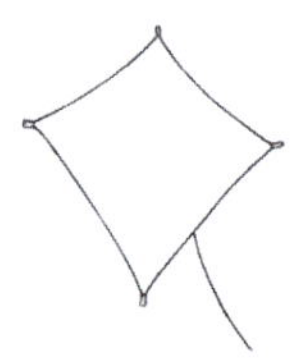

k________

4. (ake, one)

c________

5. (ead, aid)

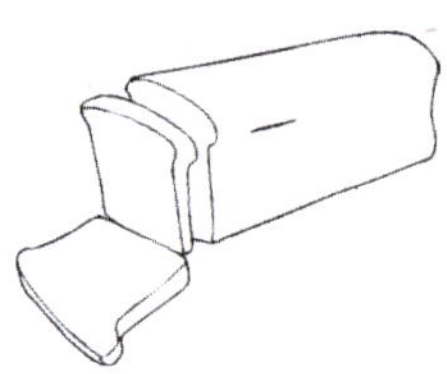

br________

6. (est, eat)

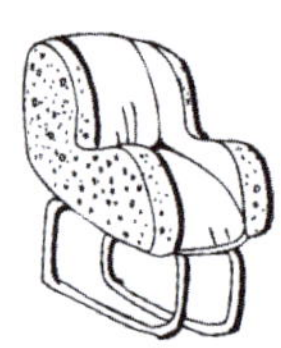

s________

Parent/Teacher Signature Date

Test

Choose the correct word in the brackets. Write it in the space.

1	I ate a bowl of (mice, rice).	1
2	Oliver baked a (cake, take) for tea.	2
3	He grabbed the lizard by the (tail, snail).	3
4	I ate all the food on my (gate, plate)	4
5	I caught a (fish, wish) in the river.	5
6	My uncle lives on a (farm, harm).	6

Total correct ______
6

Parent/Teacher Signature Date

UNIT 34

Compound words 1

Compound words are words made up of two smaller words.

Colour the correct compound word that matches each picture.

1.

blackbird	bedtime

2.

sunset	goldfish

3.

bulldog	tiptruck

4.

eggcup	butterfly

5.

football	inside

6.

waterfall	bedroom

Parent/Teacher Signature Date

UNIT 35

Compound words 2

Compound words are words made up of two smaller words.

Which word would you add to make the compound word? Write it in the space.

1. rain, black

__________bow

2. pig, cow

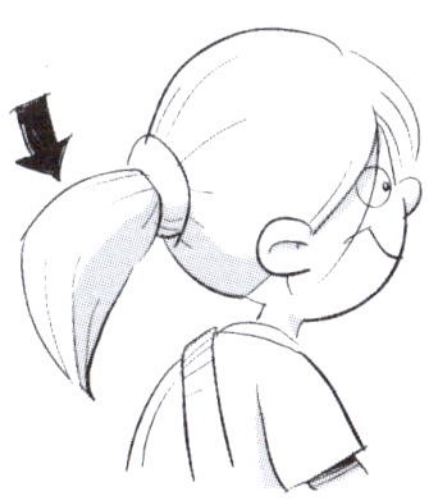

__________tail

3. box, arm

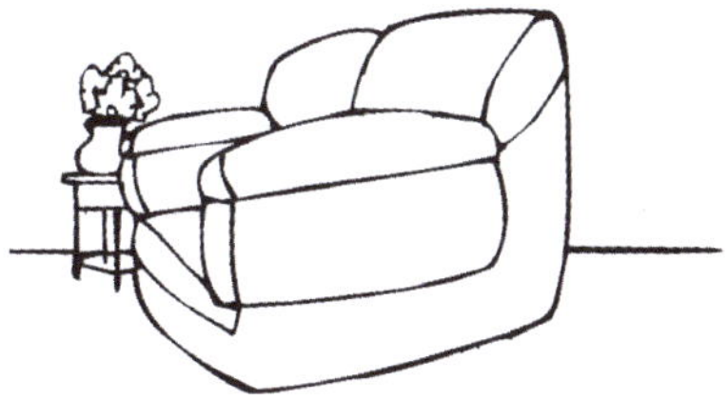

__________chair

4. foot, eye

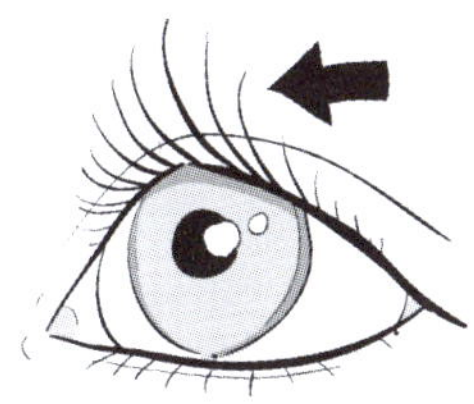

__________lash

5. shoe, star

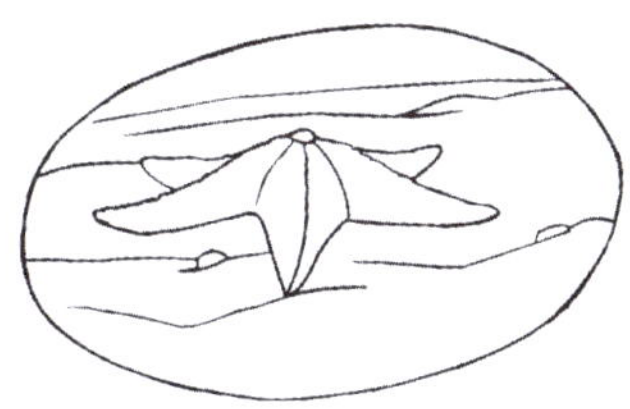

__________fish

6. bee, egg

__________cup

Parent/Teacher Signature Date

UNIT 36

Writing in code

Sometimes we can write a symbol for a letter, such as:

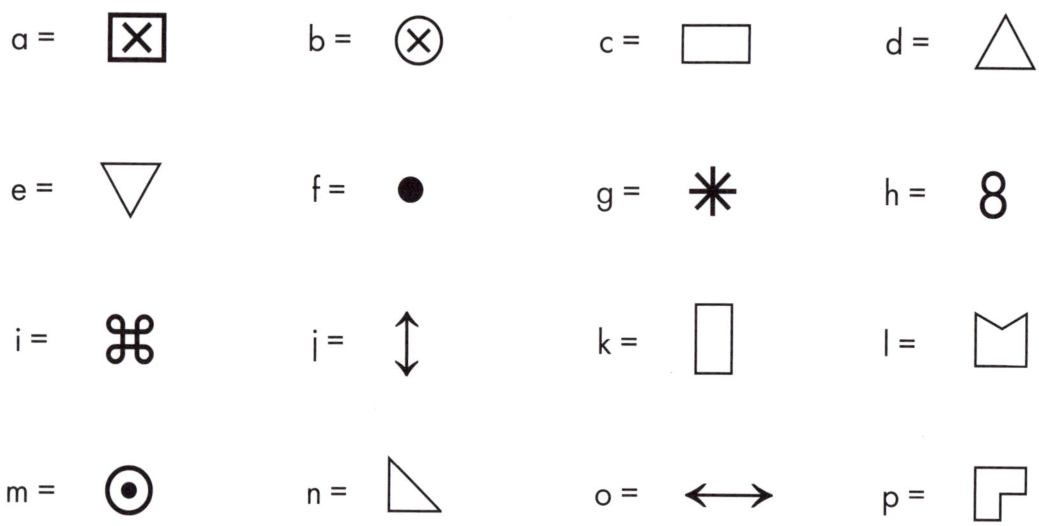

Look at each group of symbols below. Write the three letters of each word, using the code symbols above. Draw a picture for each word you make.

1.  ____________

2.  ____________

3.  ____________

4.  ____________

Parent/Teacher Signature Date

Sound patterns, ay and oy

Many words end in the letters **ay** and **oy**, as in **bay** and **boy**.

A Look at the words in the box. Write each under the correct heading below.

boy	**day**	**stay**	**hay**
play	**coy**	**joy**	**toy**

ay	oy
________________	________________
________________	________________
________________	________________
________________	________________

B Choose the correct word in the brackets. Write it in the space.

1. I did not know the (way, ray). ________________
2. The hen will (lay, stay) an egg. ________________
3. I carried the glasses on a (tray, clay). ________________
4. Joshua is a big (joy, boy). ________________

Parent/Teacher Signature Date

UNIT 38

Sound patterns, initial sh

Two letters together can form a new sound. The letters sh together are often found at the beginning of a word and are sounded as in the word **shot**.

A Write the correct word under each picture.

shark **shed** **sheep** **ship** **shell** **shoe**

1. 
____

2. 
____

3. 
____

4. 
____

5. 
____

6. 
____

B Choose the correct word in the brackets. Write it on the line.

1. I had a (flower, shower) in the bathroom. _______________
2. Tom is tall but Sam is (shoot, short). _______________
3. This knife is (sharp, show). _______________
4. On my bed there is a (sheet, shall). _______________

Parent/Teacher Signature Date

Sound patterns, final sh

Two letters together can form a new sound. The letters **sh** together are also found at the end of many words, as in the word **fish**.

A Write the correct word under each picture.

fish **bush** **dish** **crash** **wash** **brush**

1.  ______________	**2.**  ______________	**3.**  ______________
4.  ______________	**5.**  ______________	**6.**  ______________

B Choose the correct word in the brackets. Write it on the line.

1. Mike made a great (dash, rash) across the yard. ______________
2. Sam has a red (rash, mash) on his arm. ______________
3. The magic fairy gave the children a (wish, dish). ______________
4. When the fire went out there was only (ash, wash) left. ______________

Parent/Teacher Signature Date

Sound patterns, ck

Two letters together can form a new sound. The letters **ck** together make a **k** sound, as in the word **pick**.

A Write the correct word under each picture.

clock **sock** **chick** **lock** **duck** **sack**

1.  ______________	**2.** 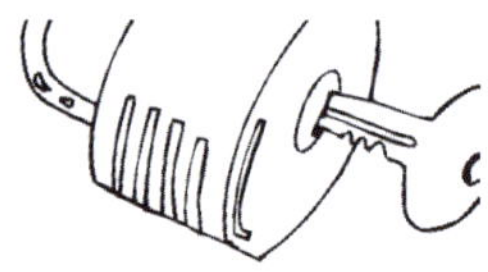 ______________	**3.**  ______________
4.  ______________	**5.**  ______________	**6.**  ______________

B Choose the correct word in the brackets. Write it on the line.

1. I like to (lick, sick) an ice-cream. ______________
2. A zebra is (black, tack) and white. ______________
3. There is a large (peck, rock) on the roadside. ______________
4. Lachlan will (lick, kick) the ball for goal. ______________

Parent/Teacher Signature Date

Sound patterns, ch

Two letters together can form a new sound. The letters **ch** together are sounded as in the word **arch**.

A Write the correct word under each picture.

chain **peach** **cheese** **beach** **cheek** **chair**

1. 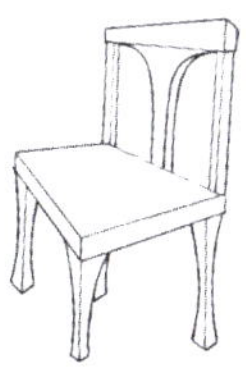 ________________	**2.**  ________________	**3.**  ________________
4.  ________________	**5.**  ________________	**6.** 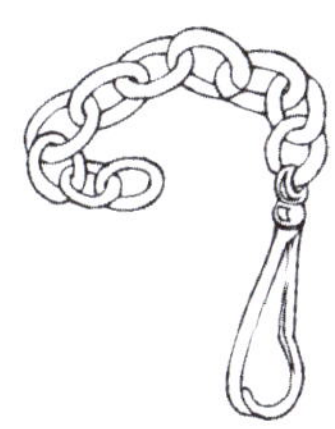 ________________

B Choose the correct word in the brackets. Write it on the line.

1. I climbed the (branch, each) of the tree. ________________
2. Tom is an adult and Mia is a (chin, child). ________________
3. I ate a red (cheery, cherry) from the tree. ________________
4. I like to (chat, rich) to people ________________

Parent/Teacher Signature   Date

Sound patterns, long and short oo

The letters **oo** together sometimes make a long sound, as in **hoot**, and sometimes they make a short sound, as in **book**.

A Write the correct long **oo** word under each picture.

broom **root** **spoon** **moon** **roof** **boot**

1. 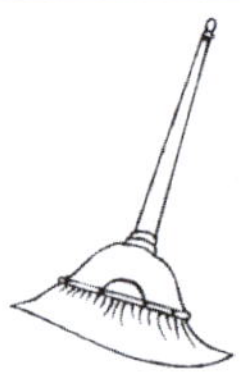 ________	**2.** 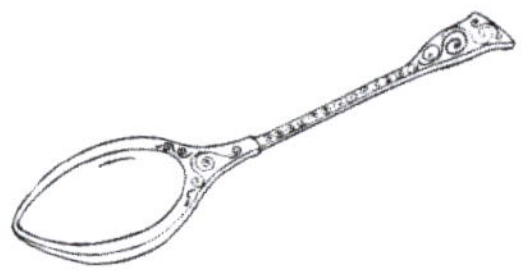 ________	**3.**  ________
4. 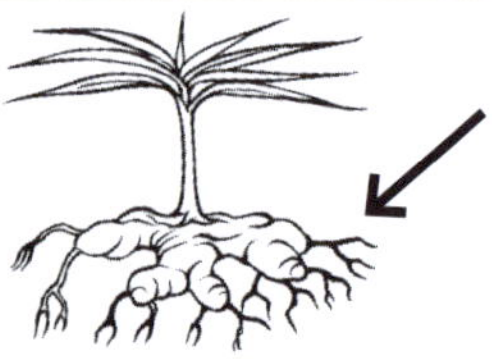 ________	**5.**  ________	**6.**  ________

B Say each short **oo** word aloud. Draw a picture for each word.

book	wool	foot
hood	hook	wood

Parent/Teacher Signature Date

Look at the pictures and think of the word for each one. Each word contains the letters **ck**, **sh** or **ch**. Write each word under the correct heading below.

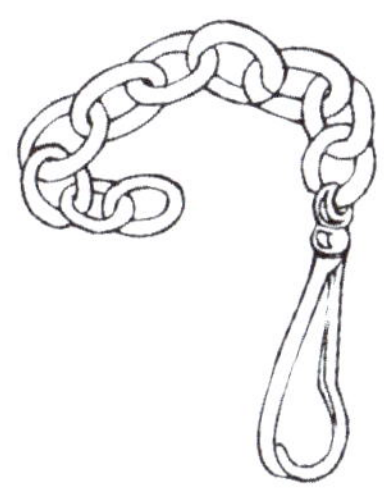		

ck	sh	ch
______________	______________	______________
______________	______________	______________

Parent/Teacher Signature Date

Test 1

Choose the correct word in the brackets. Write it in the space.

1	I saw a (ship, shep) on the sea.	1
2	The farmer fed (hey, hay) to the cows.	2
3	There was a car (crack, crash) at the corner.	3
4	We always (lok, lock) our doors.	4
5	I am sitting in a (shair, chair).	5
6	At night we can see the (muun, moon).	6

Total correct ______ / 6

Parent/Teacher Signature

Date

Test 2

From the words in the brackets on the right, find and write the word that has the same sound as the words grouped on the left. Write the word on the line.

1	boy	joy	toy	____________	(coy, hay)
2	shed	shark	ship	____________	(chest, shoe)
3	dash	wash	fish	____________	(crush, watch)
4	lock	duck	sack	____________	(fish, sock)
5	chip	chin	chain	____________	(chair, ship)
6	spoon	moon	broom	____________	(boot, leaf)

Total correct ____________ 6

Parent/Teacher Signature Date

Adding vowels 1

Vowels are the letters **a**, **e**, **i**, **o** and **u**. All words contain at least one vowel sound. Many words are made up of just three letters, two consonants (letters that are not vowels) and a vowel in between.

Look at the pictures below and write the correct vowel in the space to complete each word.

1.  m____p	**6** 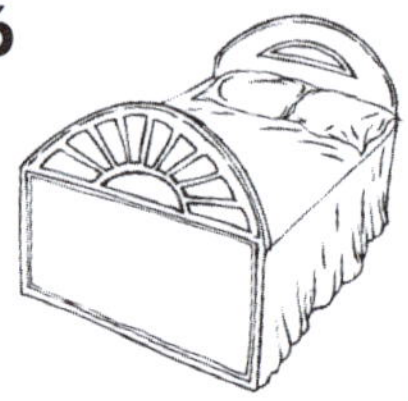 b____d	**11.**  s____n
2. 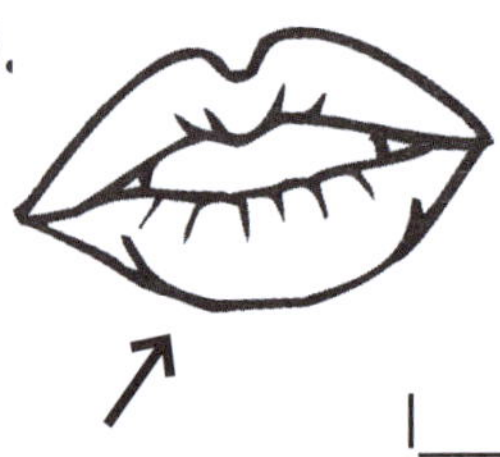 l____p	**7.** 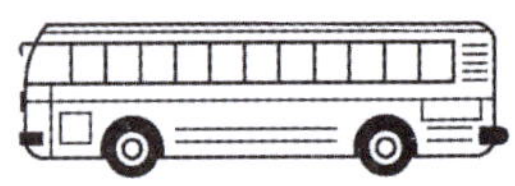 b____s	**12.**  h____t
3.  c____p	**8.**  c____w	**13.** 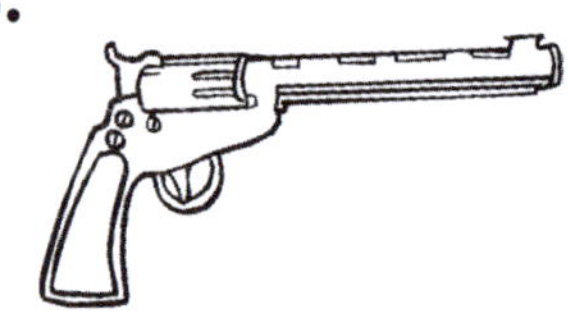 g____n
4. 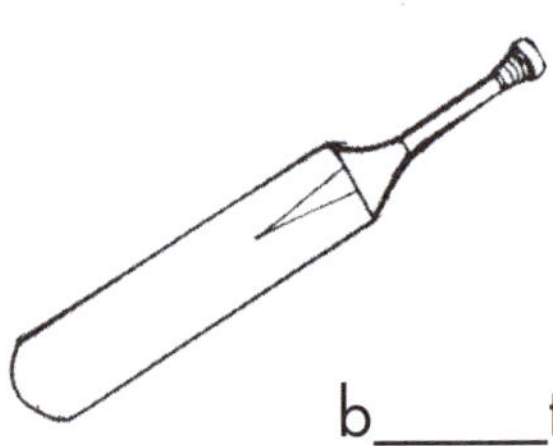 b____t	**9.**  p____n	**14.**  p____t
5. 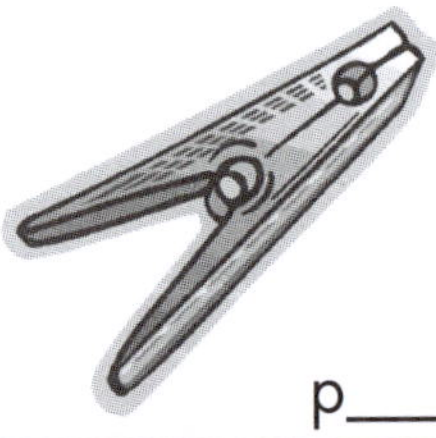 p____g	**10.** 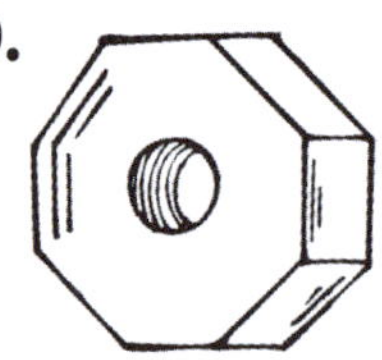 n____t	**15.**  b____y

Parent/Teacher Signature Date

UNIT 47

Adding vowels 2

Many words of more than three letters also include just one vowel.

Look at the pictures and pick which vowel – **a**, **e**, **i**, **o** or **u** – correctly completes each word.

1.  f____sh	**7.**  tr____ck	**13.** 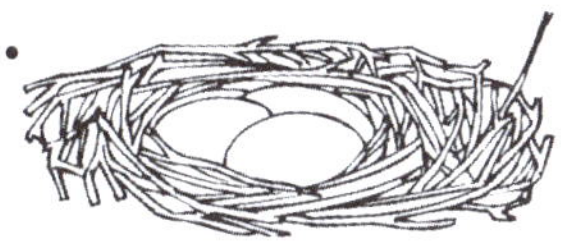 n____st
2. 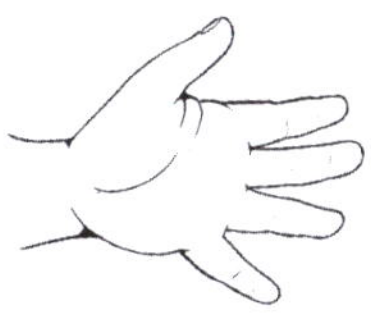 h____nd	**8.** 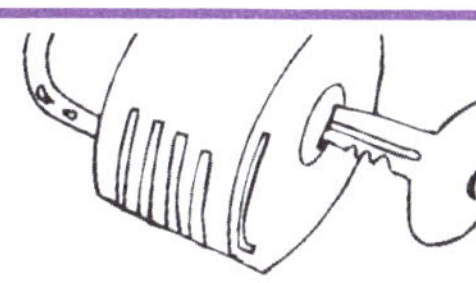 l____ck	**14.** 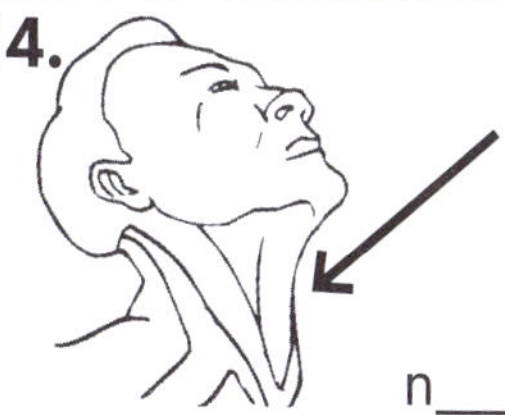 n____ck
3. 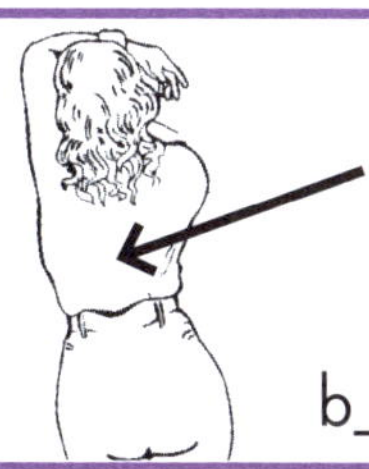 b____ck	**9.**  f____ve	**15.**  cr____b
4. 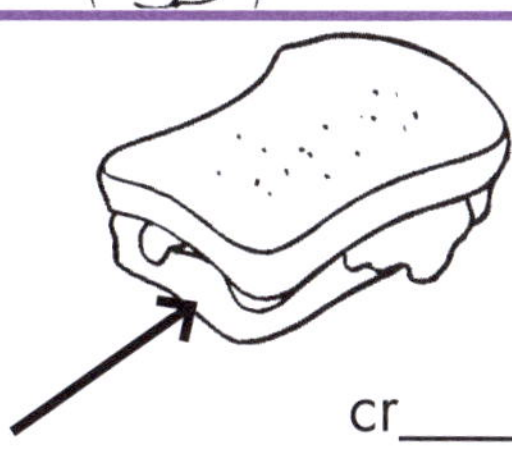 cr____st	**10.**  b____ne	**16.**  sh____p
5.  b____ll	**11.** 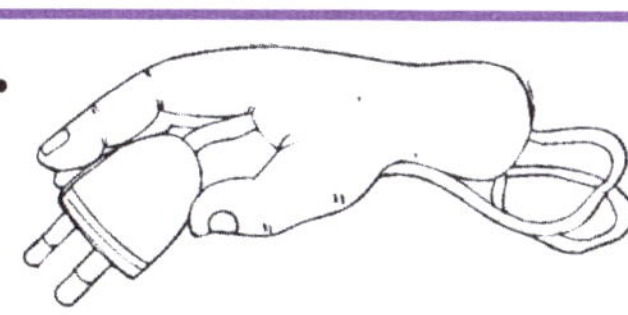 pl____g	**17.**  br____sh
6.  d____ll	**12.**  w____ve	**18.** 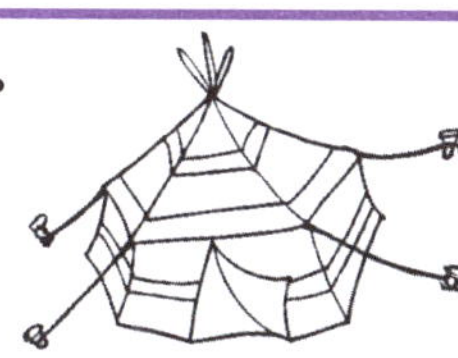 t____nt

Parent/Teacher Signature   Date

UNIT 48

Adding initial letters

Some words begin with a consonant (letters that are not vowels, such as **b**ig, and some words begin with a vowel, such as **a**nd. Look at the pictures and pick the correct letter to begin each word.

1. 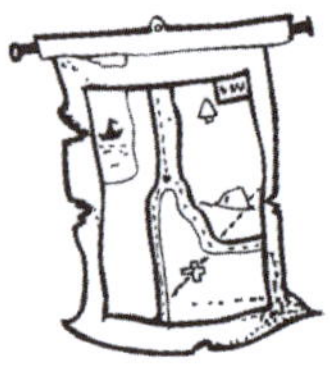 ____ap	**6.**  ____ig	**11.** 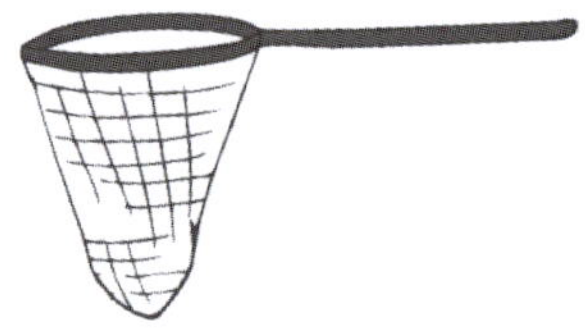 ____et
2.  ____nt	**7.**  ____gg	**12.** 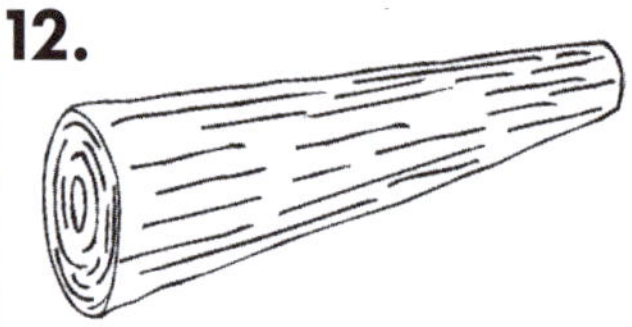 ____og
3. 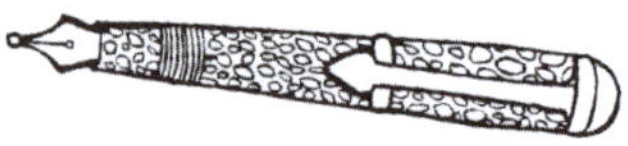 ____en	**8.**  ____an	**13.**  ____ce
4.  ____hip	**9.**  ____uck	**14.**  ____ond
5.  ____lower	**10.** 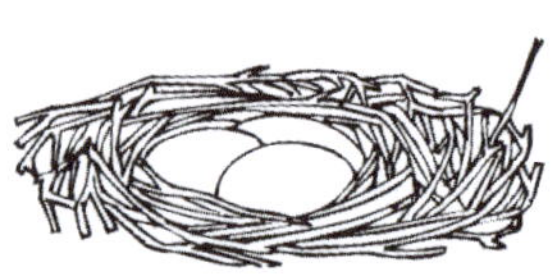 ____est	**15.**  ____ilk

Parent/Teacher Signature Date

Adding final letters

Some words end with a consonant (letters that are not vowels), such as **big**, and some words end with a vowel, such as **the**. Look at the pictures and pick the correct letter to end each word. All of these words end in a consonant.

1. 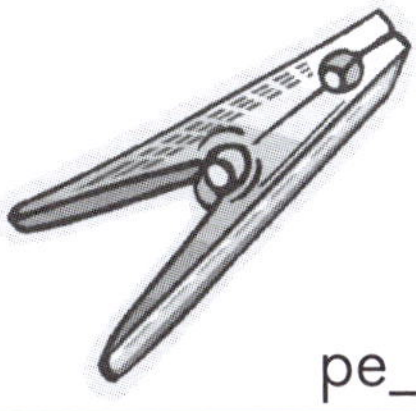 pe____	**7.**  si____	**13.** 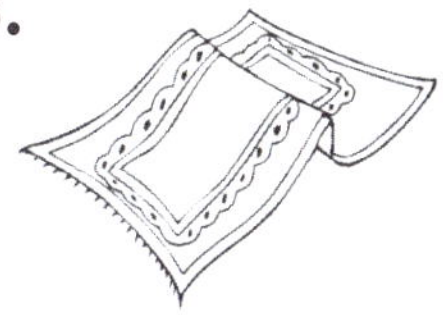 ru____
2. 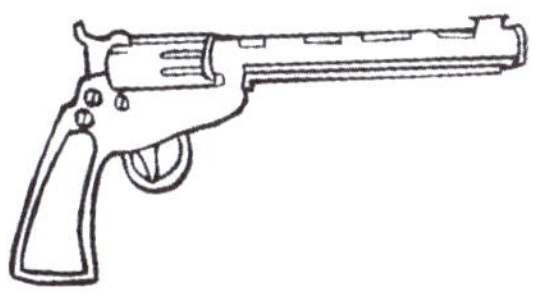 gu____	**8.** 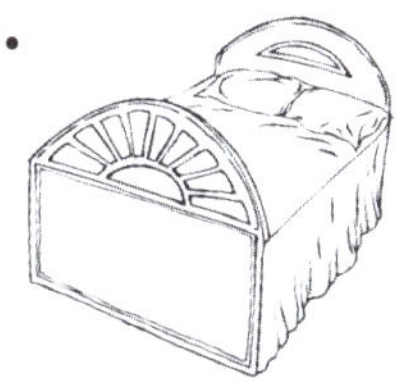 be____	**14.**  bu____
3.  cu____	**9.**  fo____	**15.** 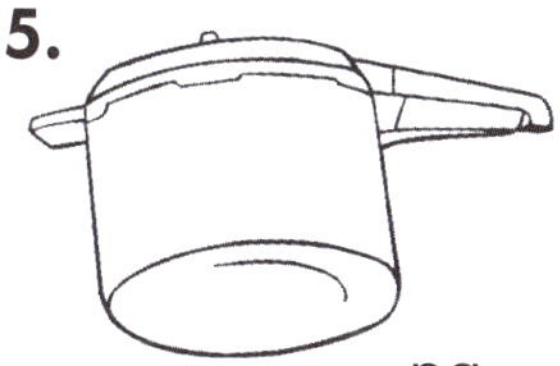 pa____
4.  ta____	**10.** 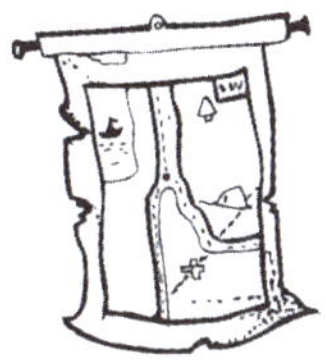 ma____	**16.**  co____
5. 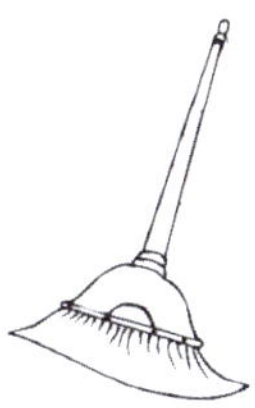 broo____	**11.**  cloc____	**17.** 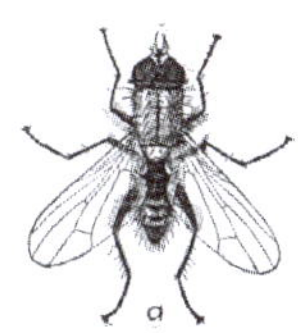 fl____
6.  cra____	**12.**  fro____	**18.** 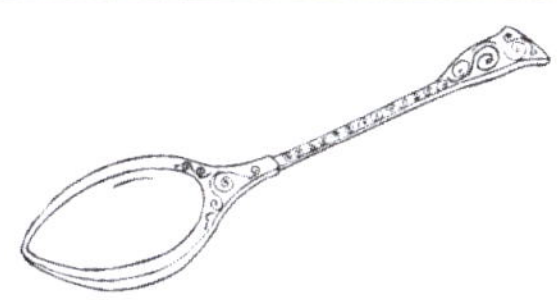 spoo____

Parent/Teacher Signature Date

UNIT 50

Revision

Look at the pictures.
Put a cross (×) in the box for those that end with **b**.
Put a tick (✓) in the box for those that end with **g**.
Put a circle (○) in the box for those that end with **m**.

1. 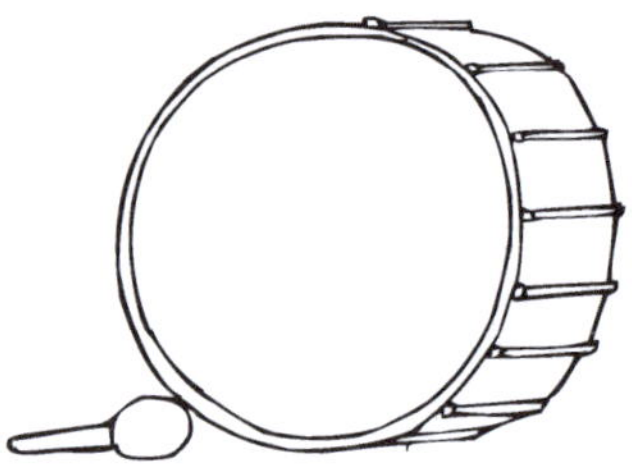	**2.** 	**3.** 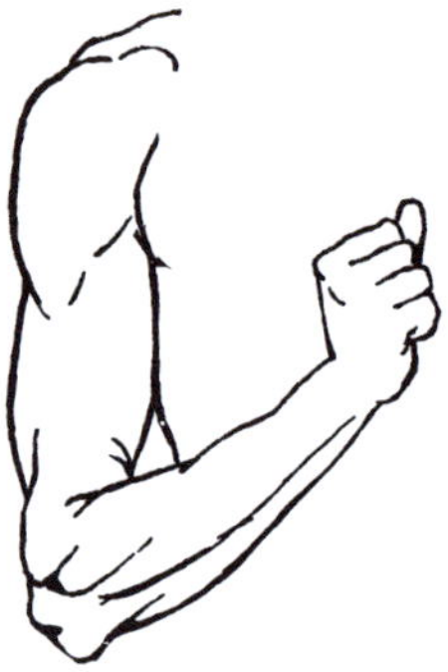
4. 	**5.** 	**6.** 

Parent/Teacher Signature Date

Test

Choose the correct word in the brackets. Write it in the space.

1 I sleep in a (bed, bad). [ ] 1

2 At the beach I saw a (crib, crab). [ ] 2

3 Jack fell on his (beck, back). [ ] 3

4 A (ship, chip) sailed across the sea. [ ] 4

5 I ate my food with a (spook, spoon). [ ] 5

6 There was a (frog, from) in the garden. [ ] 6

Total correct ______ / 6

Parent/Teacher Signature Date

UNIT 52

Anagrams 1

An anagram is a word that is made up from the jumbled-up letters of another word, such as **tip** and **pit**.

Rearrange the letters of these words to make a word that matches the picture.

1.

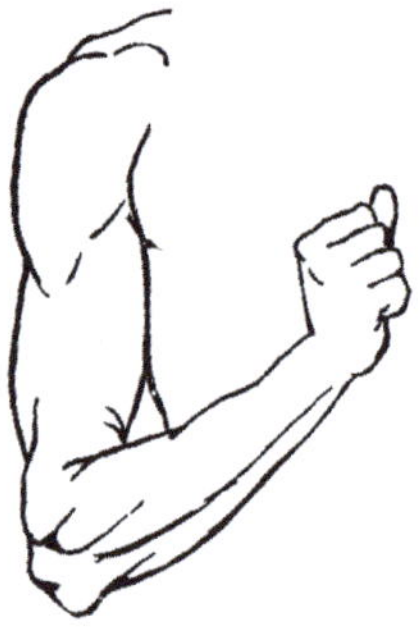

ram ______________

4.

act ______________

2.

tan ______________

5.

god ______________

3.

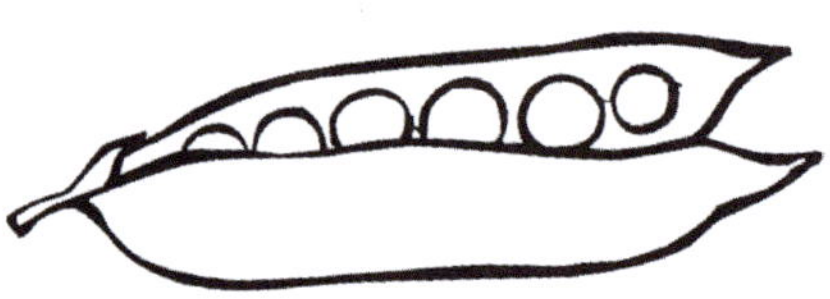

ape ______________

6.

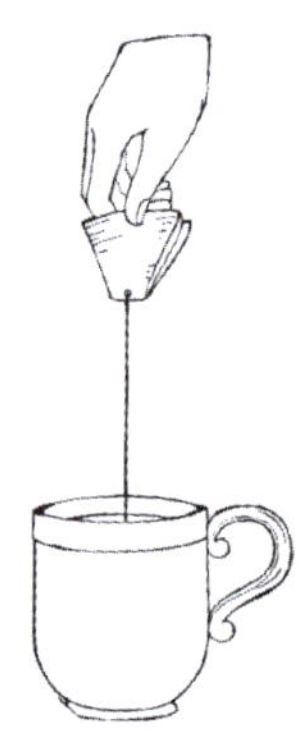

eat ______________

Parent/Teacher Signature Date

UNIT 53

Anagrams 2

An anagram is a word that is made up from the jumbled-up letters of another word, such as **tip** and **pit**.

Rearrange the letters of these words to make a word that matches the picture.

1.

pat ____________

2.

low ____________

3.

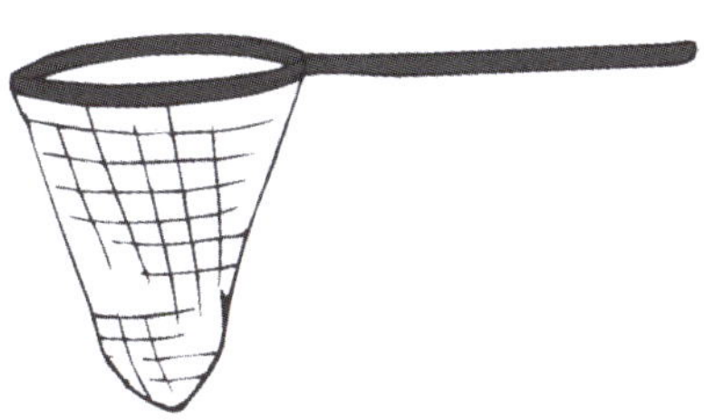

ten ____________

4.

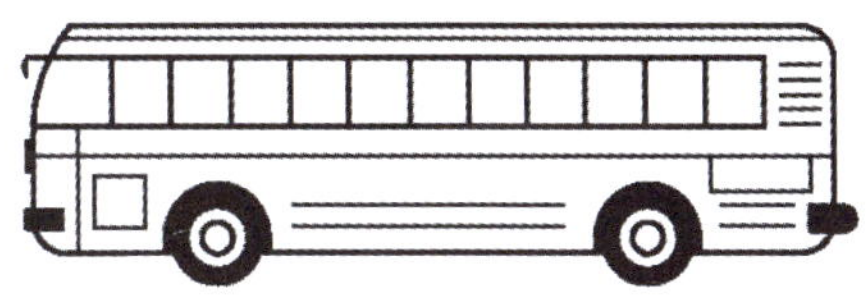

sub ____________

5.

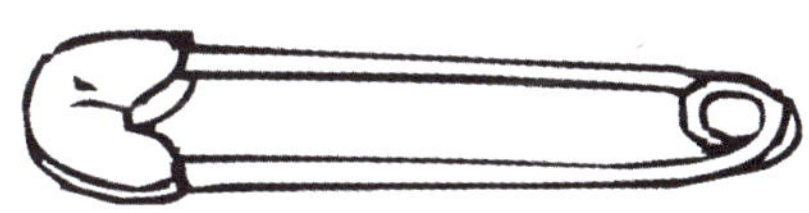

nip ____________

6.

tar ____________

Parent/Teacher Signature   Date

UNIT 54

Find the words

A The cramped words in the box all begin with **b**. Find each word and write it correctly on the line. Draw a picture for each word.

busbatbirdboxboyball

1. ________	**2.** ________	**3.** ________
4. ________	**5.** ________	**6.** ________

B The cramped words in the box all begin with **c**. Find each word and write it correctly on the line. Draw a picture for each word.

capcatcarcotcowcake

1. ________	**2.** ________	**3.** ________
4. ________	**5.** ________	**6.** ________

Parent/Teacher Signature Date

r-Influenced vowels, ar

When the letter **a** is followed by the letter **r** it makes a long **ar** sound, as in **bar** and **tar**.

A Write the correct word from the box to match each picture.

car **arm** **card** **jar** **dart** **star**

1. 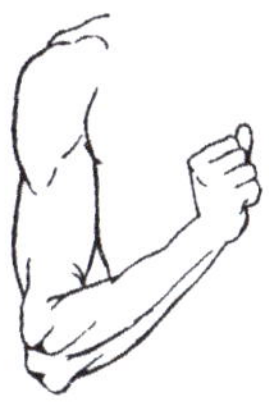 ____________	**2.**  ____________	**3.** 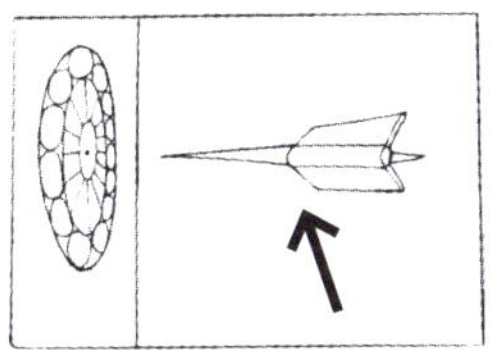 ____________
4.  ____________	**5.**  ____________	**6.**  ____________

B Choose the correct word in the brackets and write it on the line.

1. At night it becomes (dart, dark). ____________
2. A dog can (bark, yard). ____________
3. You will see animals on a (start, farm). ____________
4. We went for a picnic in the (lark, park). ____________
5. The boys (are, art) coming. ____________

Parent/Teacher Signature Date

UNIT 56

r-Influenced vowels, or

When the letter **o** is followed by the letter **r** it makes a long **or** sound, as in **for** and **port**.

A Write the correct word from the box under each picture.

horse **fork** **corn** **torch** **story** **storm**

1.	2.	3.
 ____________	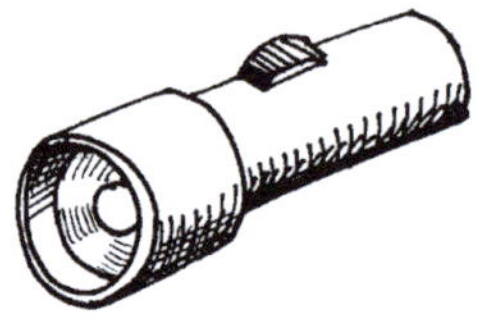 ____________	 ____________
4.	**5.**	**6.**
 ____________	 ____________	 ____________

B Choose the correct word in the brackets and write it on the line.

1. John is tall but Bill is (short, fort). ____________
2. I like to play different (sorts, sports). ____________
3. Tom has a (sore, pore) eye. ____________
4. We will meet at the (morning, corner) of the school. ________

Parent/Teacher Signature Date

Sound patterns, oa

The letters **oa** together make a long **o** sound, as in **coast** and **float**.

A Write the correct word from the box under its picture.

boat **coat** **goat** **loaf** **road** **soap**

1.  ______________	**2.**  ______________	**3.**  ______________
4. 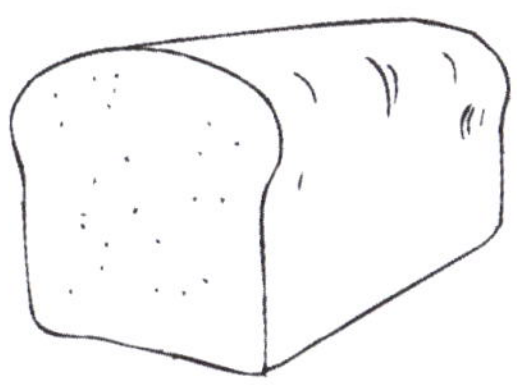 ______________	**5.** 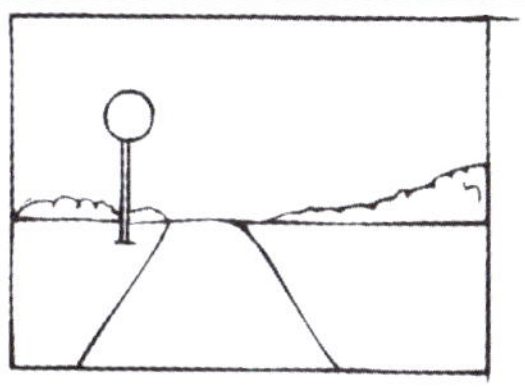 ______________	**6.**  ______________

B Read the story. Find and write all the **oa** words.

One day a toad was near a load of oats that were being taken by coach to the coast. It began to rain and the water started to soak the ground. Lots of things began to float past so the toad began to croak.

1. ______________ 4. ______________ 7. ______________

2. ______________ 5. ______________ 8. ______________

3. ______________ 6. ______________ 9. ______________

Parent/Teacher Signature Date

UNIT 58

Sound patterns, ai

The letters **ai** together make a long **a** sound, as in **fail** and **rail**.

A Write the words from the box under the correct picture.

chain **train** **nail** **snail** **sail** **tail**

1. 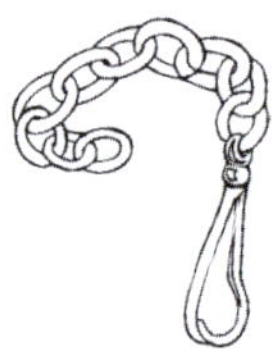 ______________	**2.** 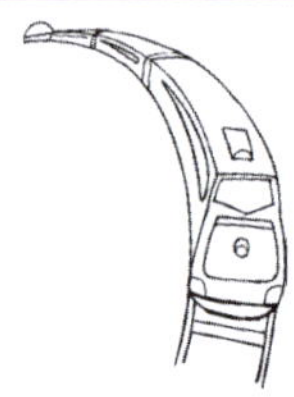 ______________	**3.**  ______________
4. 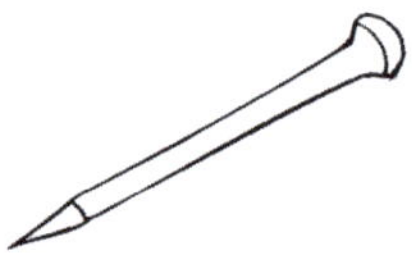 ______________	**5.** 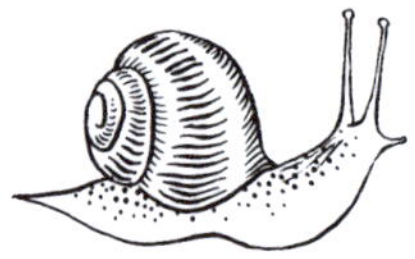 ______________	**6.**  ______________

B Read the story and circle all the words with an **ai** sound. Write them on the lines.

The maid collected the mail. Soon it began to rain and the water ran down the drain of the house. We hoped it would not hail because that would harm the paint.

1. ______________ 4. ______________

2. ______________ 5. ______________

3. ______________ 6. ______________

Parent/Teacher Signature Date

Sound patterns, ee

UNIT 59

The letters ee together make a long e sound, as in **free** and **fee**.

A Circle the correct word under each picture.

1.	2.	3.
	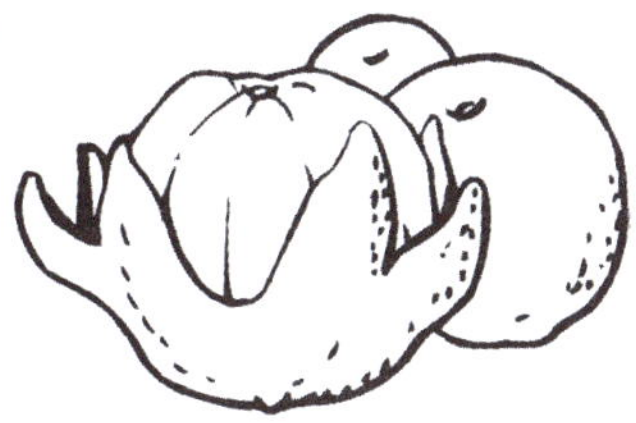	3
bee fee	peer peel	thee three
4.	**5.**	**6.**
		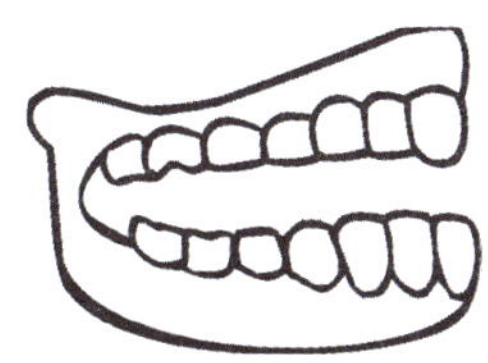
seed deed	tree tee	teeth weed

B Read the sentence and circle all the words that contain ee. Write them on the lines.

After we had a sleep last week we went down the street to meet a lady who I had seen at the green house.

1. ______________________ 4. ______________________

2. ______________________ 5. ______________________

3. ______________________ 6. ______________________

Parent/Teacher Signature Date

Consonant blends

A Many words begin with two consonants that blend together, such as **fl** (**flat**), **br** (**broom**), **cl** (**clap**), **cr** (**crown**), **dr** (**drain**) and **fr** (**from**). Write the correct word from the box below each picture.

flag brush cloud crab drum frog

1.  ______________	**2.**  ______________	**3.** 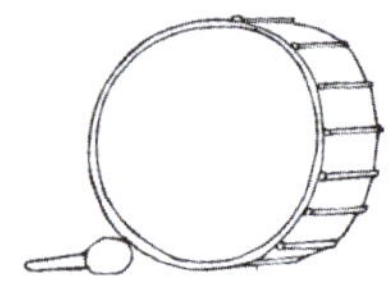 ______________
4.  ______________	**5.**  ______________	**6.**  ______________

B A consonant blend can also be a word ending, such as **st** (**post**), **nd** (**wind**), **nt** (**mint**), **lt** (**wilt**), **mp** (**romp**) and **lk** (**bulk**). Write the correct word from the box under each picture.

nest hand ant belt lamp milk

1. 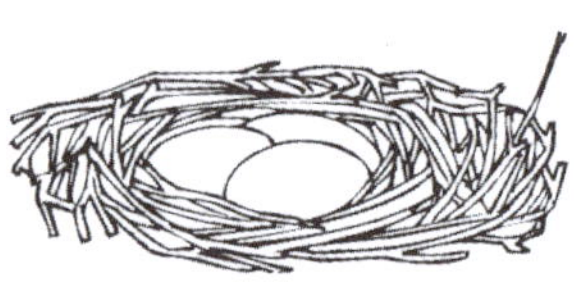 ______________	**2.**  ______________	**3.** 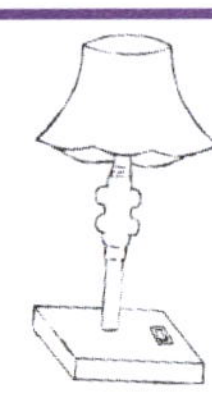 ______________
4. 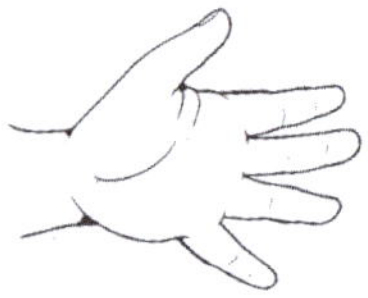 ______________	**5.** 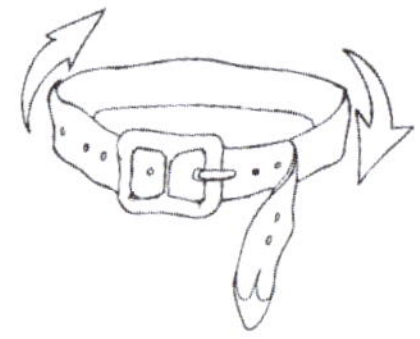 ______________	**6.**  ______________

Parent/Teacher Signature   Date

Look at the pictures. Write the word for each one under the correct heading below — **ar**, **or** or **oa**.

ar	or	oa
______	______	______
______	______	______
______	______	______
______	______	______

Parent/Teacher Signature Date

Test 1

Choose the correct word in the brackets. Write it in the space.

1 We saw a (star, staar) in the sky. [1]

2 I eat with a knife and (fawk, fork). [2]

3 On the farm we saw a (gote, goat). [3]

4 The (snail, snale) ate the lettuce leaf. [4]

5 The number after two is (thee, three). [5]

6 At the beach I saw a (crab, grab). [6]

Total correct ______ / 6

Parent/Teacher Signature   Date

Test 2

The underlined word in each sentence is spelled wrongly. Write it correctly in the space.

1 I wore a <u>cote</u> to school. [1]

2 The dog bit its <u>taill</u>. [2]

3 I put the apple <u>pele</u> in the bin. [3]

4 A <u>grab</u> bit my toe at the beach. [4]

5 The teacher read us a <u>stori</u>. [5]

6 I went for a ride in a <u>cawr</u>. [6]

Total correct ______ / 6

Parent/Teacher Signature   Date

UNIT 64

Word building, changing letters

Change the first letter of each word to make a new word that matches the drawings. Write the new word on the line. The first one has been done for you.

1. pest
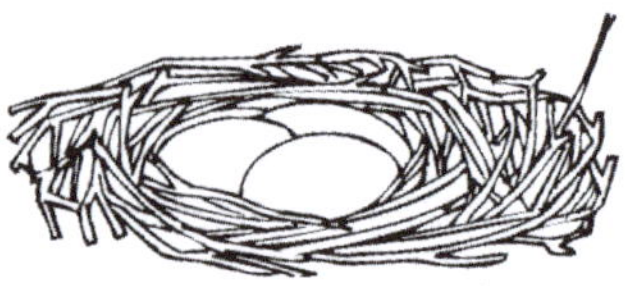
n est

2. bone

___one

3. block

___lock

4. clag

___lag

5. tear

___ear

6. noon

___oon

7. house

___ouse

8. cell

___ell

9. coat

___oat

10. sing

___ing

11. pine

___ine

12. save

___ave

Parent/Teacher Signature Date

Word building, adding letters

Add a letter to each word to make a new word to match the picture. Write the new word on the line. The first one has been done for you.

1. hip

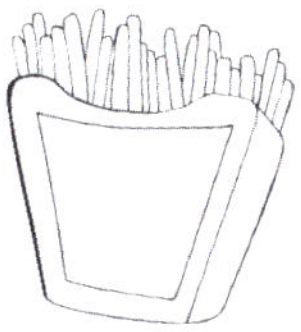

chip

2. sell

______

3. love

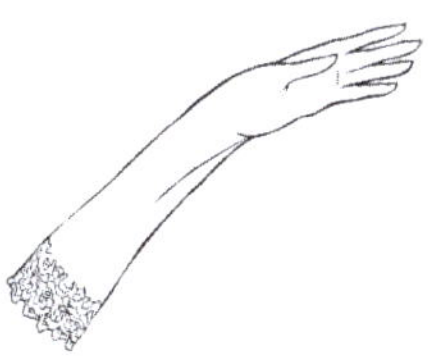

______

4. ice

______

5. fog

______

6. wig

______

7. sat

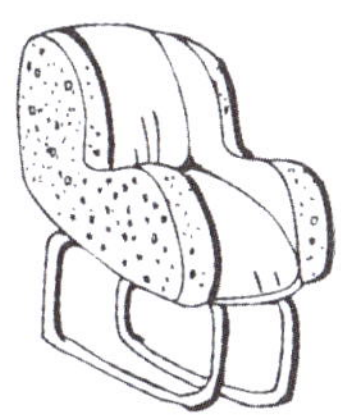

______

8. sea

______

9. seep

______

10. hose

______

11. wing

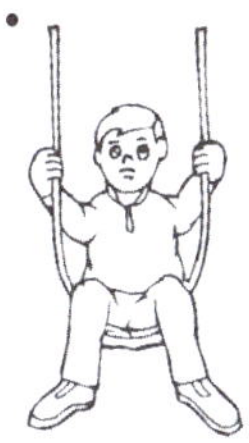

______

12. fat

______

Parent/Teacher Signature   Date

UNIT 66

Word building, initial letters

Make a word by using the first letter of each picture. Write the letters under the pictures and then write the word in the final box. The first one has been done for you.

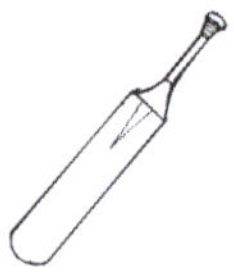  

1. b + a + g = bag

2. ☐ + ☐ + ☐ + ☐ = ☐

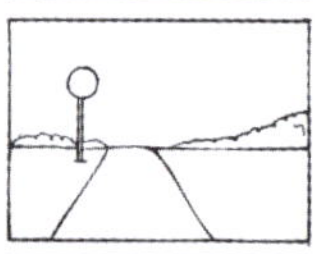   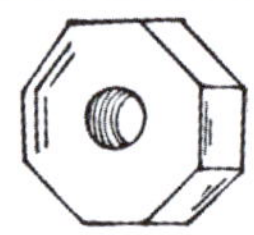

3. ☐ + ☐ + ☐ + ☐ = ☐

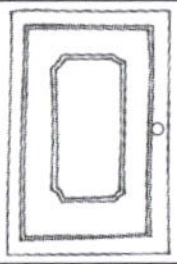   

4. ☐ + ☐ + ☐ + ☐ = ☐

 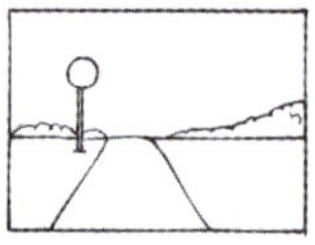  

5. ☐ + ☐ + ☐ + ☐ = ☐

 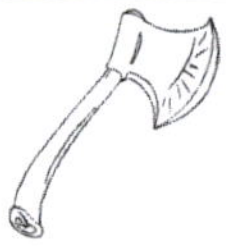 10 

6. ☐ + ☐ + ☐ + ☐ = ☐

Parent/Teacher Signature Date

Word building, word sums

Add the word pieces to make a word. Write the word on the line and draw a picture for each one.

Example: h + en = hen

1. sh + ell = ________________	**6.** h + ou + se = ________________
2. w + in + dow = ________________	**7.** g + ar + den = ________________
3. br + i + ck = ________________	**8.** r + abb + it = ________________
4. f + in + ger = ________________	**9.** d + on + key = ________________
5. ch + ick + en = ________________	**10.** pl + a + nt = ________________

Parent/Teacher Signature Date

Revision

A Add the first or last letter to make a word that matches the picture.

1.

sno______

2.

mil______

3.

coa______

4.

______tar

5.

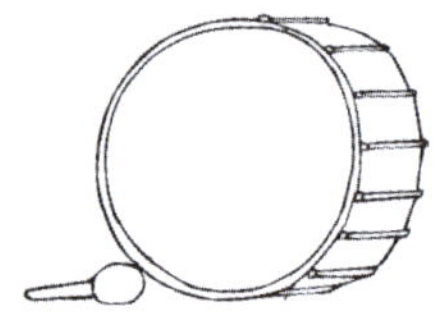

______rum

6.

______ouse

B Join the word pieces in Box B to a word piece in Box A. Write the word and draw a picture for each one.

Box A	**Box B**	
1. tr	oon	________________
2. sh	own	________________
3. sp	ip	________________
4. cr	uck	________________

Parent/Teacher Signature Date

Test

Choose the correct word in the brackets. Write it in the space.

1 It was cold and it began to (glow, snow). [1]

2 At the beach I found a (shell, chell). [2]

3 Our (howse, house) has a red roof. [3]

4 We rowed the (boat, coat) across the lake. [4]

5 The (block, clock) was ten minutes slow. [5]

6 A big (save, wave) hit the boat. [6]

Total correct ______ / 6

Parent/Teacher Signature   Date

UNIT 70

Reading and drawing

Choose the correct word and draw a picture.

1. This is a (bed, red).	4. This is a (lock, black) cat.
2. This is a (yellow, lellow) bus.	5. This is a (green, seen) truck.
3. This is a (brown, town) fox.	6. This is a (blue, true) dress.

Parent/Teacher Signature Date

Jumbled letters

Unjumble the letters of the word to write the word that matches the picture.

1.

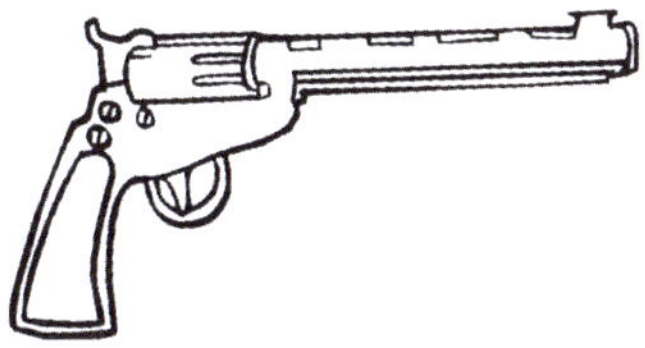

gnu ________________

2.

6

xis ________________

3.

mta ________________

4.

mpo ________________

5.

gip ________________

6.

nus ________________

Parent/Teacher Signature   Date

Find the words

A The cramped words in the box all begin with **d**. Find each word and write it correctly on the line. Draw a picture for each word.

dogdishdolldoorduckdrum

1. ________	**2.** ________	**3.** ________
4. ________	**5.** ________	**6.** ________

B These cramped words all begin with **t**. Find each word and write it correctly on the line. Draw a picture for each word.

tailtreetoytaptenttoe

1. ________	**2.** ________	**3.** ________
4. ________	**5.** ________	**6.** ________

Parent/Teacher Signature Date

Review

A Write the words in the box under their headings below. Look for the letter patterns.

toy	wall	stay
play	boy	call

oy	all	ay
____	____	____
____	____	____

B Circle the word that has a different letter pattern for each row.

1.	bone	cone	duck	done
2.	deer	hook	look	book
3.	bark	dark	book	park
4.	work	fork	pork	crab
5.	bell	shoe	fell	well
6.	dish	wish	fish	truck

Parent/Teacher Signature Date

Test 1

Choose the correct word in the brackets and write it in the space.

1 I put the papers in the (bin, pin). [1]

2 There is a (map, sap) on the wall. [2]

3 I bounced the (ball, bill) near the goal. [3]

4 A fish has a (fin, tin). [4]

5 My brother has a new (toy, coy). [5]

6 I saw a (chip, ship) on the ocean. [6]

Total correct ______ / 6

Parent/Teacher Signature Date

Test 2

Choose the correct set of letters from the brackets and write it on the line.

1 We get wool from a sh____p. (oo, ee)

2 Our cat jumped up on the r____f. (oo, ee)

3 I sat in a ____air. (sh, ch)

4 Ethan is feeling si____. (ck, ch)

5 Chloe has a red ra____ on her arm. (sh, ch)

6 I saw a ____ar in the sky. (sl, st)

Total correct ______ / 6

Parent/Teacher Signature Date

Test 3

The underlined word is spelled wrongly. Write the correct spelling in the space.

1 I like to read a <u>boock</u>. [ ] 1

2 We get <u>milc</u> from cows. [ ] 2

3 Oliver can play a <u>drom</u>. [ ] 3

4 I saw a <u>flarg</u> flying on the pole. [ ] 4

5 Sophie is wearing a warm <u>cowt</u> to school. [ ] 5

6 I like to eat <u>cawn</u>. [ ] 6

Total correct ______ / 6

Parent/Teacher Signature Date

Useful Words

and	dig	has	mat	pug	sit
bad	din	hat	may	pup	six
bag	dip	hat	men	put	sun
bat	dob	hem	met	rag	tan
bee	dog	hen	mix	ram	tap
big	dot	her	mop	ran	ten
bin	dug	hid	mud	rap	the
box	fad	him	net	rat	tig
bun	fan	his	nip	red	tin
bus	far	hit	nod	rib	tog
but	fat	hog	not	rid	top
can	fig	hop	nun	rig	tub
cap	fit	hot	nut	rob	tug
car	fox	hut	pad	rot	van
cat	fox	jam	pal	rub	wag
cot	fun	jar	pan	rug	war
cow	fur	jet	pat	run	wet
cup	gas	jog	peg	sad	wig
cut	get	jug	pen	sap	win
dab	got	log	pet	sat	yes
dad	gum	mad	pie	saw	yet
den	gun	map	pig	set	zap
did	had	mar	pin	sip	zip

Initial consonant blends

bl	black	blew	block	blow	blue		
br	brave	brick	bring	broke	broom	brown	brush
cl	clap	clip	clock	clown	clump		
cr	crab	crash	cross	crust	cry		
dr	dress	drip	drop	drum	dry		
fl	flag	flat	flew	flow	fly		
fr	free	frock	frog	from	fry		
gr	grab	grade	grip	grow	grub		
pl	plan	plane	plant	play			
pr	pram	pray	prick	press			
sh	shed	ship	shop	shot	shut		
sk	skid	skin	skip	sky			
sp	space	speck	spell	spin	spoon	spot	spy
st	stab	star	stay	step	stick	street	sty
tr	tram	trap	tree	trip	try		

Final consonant blends

ck	back	pack	sack	tack	neck	peck	
	lick	pick	sick	tick	sock	duck	luck
ft	raft	left	gift	lift	soft	tuft	
ll	ball	call	fall	hall	mall	tall	wall
	bell	fell	sell	tell	well	yell	
	bill	hill	fill	kill	pill	till	will
	doll	roll	toll	bull	dull	full	pull
lt	belt	felt	melt	tilt	bolt		
mp	lamp	stamp	limp	bump	jump	lump	pump
nd	and	band	hand	land	sand	stand	wand
	bend	end	lend	mend	send	pond	
nk	bank	plank	drink	ink	sink	wink	
nt	ant	plant	bent	sent	tent	went	
sh	dash	lash	rash	wash	dish	fish	wish
sk	ask	mask	desk	risk	dusk	tusk	
st	fast	best	nest	list	lost	most	dust

WINK: Words I Need to Know

For many people, some words are often hard to spell. Record words you are having difficulty with on this page.

Word	Word	Word

Some Tips for Learning to Spell

Spelling can seem really hard sometimes. There are so many different words and rules for spelling them. Follow these tips to help you learn and improve your spelling.

★ When you read a story you might notice that some words contain the same letter patterns. Look at this story:

> One morning a tall boy looked in a box trying to find a rubber ball and a soft stuffed toy fox he wanted to play with out on the grass, but all he could find was an old brass horn.

Can you see words that have the same letters or sounds? Remembering these pattterns can help you become a better speller.

★ When you read a story you find many interesting words. Think about what makes these words a little different from others. For example, think of the words **queue** and **hijinks**. How do they seem different from other words?

★ Always try to say words correctly. It is a **river**, not a **riva**, and a **teacher**, not a **teacha**. We go **swimming**, not **swimmen**, and we go **climbing** trees, not **climen** trees.

★ When you are writing a story and don't really know how to spell a word, write the first letter and then put a dash. Ask your teacher or parents to help you spell it, or use a dictionary to check and write the word yourself. For example, you might write: Jack was chased by the g______. And later you can complete your sentence:
Jack was chased by the giant.

★ For words that give you trouble, write them on the WINK page so you will remember the words you need to know. This can be your own little spelling dictionary.

★ If the word tricks you again, LOOK at the word, COVER it up and try to WRITE it from memory. Then CHECK it. Keep doing this until you are really sure how to spell the word.

★ The best tip is to really try hard so you become tops at spelling. Read as much as you can and take care when you write a story that the words you write are correct.

Assessment

	✓	×
Displays an interest in words and their meanings.		
Spells basic words correctly.		
Is aware some words contain similar sounds (hat, cat) or similar letter patterns (grub, grin).		
Uses a variety of methods in attempting to spell different words.		
Uses aids for spelling (word lists, simple dictionary).		

	✓	×
Is prepared to review and proofread own writing attempts.		
Has a continual determination to improve skills.		
Has a good working knowledge of sound units, letter patterns and word meanings.		
Understands that the words we use can be grouped into sentences of meaning.		

Comments

Areas of strength: ______________________________

____

Areas of difficulty: ______________________________

____

Future needs or steps to be undertaken: ______________________________

____

____

Parent/Teacher Signature ______________________ Date ____________

Glossary of terms

anagram
The letters of a *word* or words that can make another word when jumbled up.
Example: **ram** and **arm**

compound word
A *word* made up of two or more smaller words, often developing first as a hyphenated word.
Example: **butter** + **fly** = **butterfly**

consonant
A letter in which the air is in some way impeded when pronounced. There are 21 consonants in the alphabet, all the letters that are not *vowels*.

consonant blend
When two or more *consonants* come together to blend a sound. Examples: **stick**, **sky**, **brown**, **straw.**
Consonant blends may be initial blends (**frog**), medial (middle) blends (**blister**), or final blends (**stamp**).

digraph
A combination of letters that represents a single sound. There are *consonant* digraphs and *vowel* digraphs. Common consonant digraphs include **sh**, **ch**, **th** and **wh**. (Consonant digraphs at the beginning of a word are called an onset; vowel digraphs are also called diphthongs.)

homophone
A word that is pronounced the same as another word, but each word has a different spelling and a different meaning.
Examples: **bear** (a furry animal) and **bare** (naked); **sure** (certain) and **shore** (coastline)

letter pattern
A letter sequence that functions as a unit and is related to a consistent category of sound.
Example: **one** = **bone**, **cone**, **tone**

long vowel
The sound of a *vowel* (**a**, **e**, **i**, **o**, **u**) that says its letter name, or is an *r-influenced vowel*.
Examples: **same**, **bacon**, **far**, **concrete**, **fever**, **fine**, **rival**, **fir**, **cone**, **robot**, **core**, **cute**, **student**, **purr**

phonics
The systematic relationship between letters and sounds.

plural
More than one. Most words make their plurals by adding an **s**. However, there are other ways to make the plurals of words.
Examples: **girl**, **girls**; **watch**, **watches**; **city**, **cities**; **piano**, **pianos**; **knife**, **knives**; **tooth**, **teeth**; **mouse**, **mice**

r-influenced vowel
A *vowel* sound that is determined by the letter **r** following it.
Example: The **a** in **far** is a *long vowel* sound but the **a** in **fad** is a *short vowel* sound.

short vowel
The sound of a *vowel* (**a**, **e**, **i**, **o** and **u**) that is clipped — a short sound. It is sometimes said short vowel sounds are the "baby" sounds.
Examples: **bat**, **bet**, **bit**, **bottle**, **but**

syllable
A sound unit that includes only one sounded *vowel*. The vowel may be preceded or followed by several *consonants*. Words can be divided into their syllables. This is a useful spelling technique. Example: **development** = **de** / **vel** / **op** / **ment**

vowel
A letter in which the air passes through the mouth without obstruction when pronounced. The letters **a**, **e**, **i**, **o** and **u** are vowels. Note: **y** does the work of the vowels **i** and **e** in words such as **cry** (long **i**), **mystery** (short **i**) and **weary** (long **e**).

word
A unit of meaning. A word may be a simple *syllable* or a combination of syllables. A word may contain smaller units of meaning within it.

Answers, Class 1

Unit 1
1. butterfly ×
2. grasshopper ✓
3. ball ×
4. bee ×
5. button ×
6. grass ✓

Unit 2
1. frog ×
2. hat ✓
3. fish ×
4. hen ✓
5. horse ✓
6. fox ×

Unit 3
1. caterpillar ×
2. cow ×
3. dog ✓
4. dragonfly ✓
5. crayon ×
6. duck ✓

Unit 4
1. jar ×
2. leggo ✓
3. lizard ✓
4. lamb ✓
5. juggler ×
6. lollipop ✓

Unit 5
1. moon ×
2. nut ✓
3. mosquito ×
4. milk ×
5. nose ✓
6. number ✓

Unit 6
1. pig ×
2. rooster ✓
3. pear ×
4. rabbit ✓
5. pie ×
6. robot ✓

Unit 7 Revision
1. bone
2. gun
3. hat
4. jug
5. net
6. duck

Unit 8 Test 1
1. book
2. bed
3. fox
4. cat
5. jug
6. nine

Unit 9 Test 2
1. pie
2. hat
3. dog
4. car
5. ladder
6. five

Unit 10
1. f
2. i
3. h
4. j
5. a
6. s
7. g
8. i and j

Unit 11
Short words:
us
on
I
log
rat
is
the
off
of
it
Long words:
mother
apple
football
computer
asleep
played
automobile
buckets
winter
history

Unit 12
1. pigs
2. trees
3. stars
4. books
5. clocks
6. hats
7. balls
8. birds
9. peas
10. ants

Unit 13
A
1. toys
2. shops
3. flowers
4. keys
5. hens
6. chairs

B
1. rats
2. beds
3. eggs
4. cows

Unit 14 Revision
One:
day
flower
bone
toy
girl
pig
More than one:
toys
girls
pigs
bones
days
flowers

Unit 15 Test 1
1. dogs
2. cows
3. flower
4. bone
5. toys
6. chairs

Unit 16
1. sun
2. sea
3. tail
4. four
5. two
6. won

Unit 17
1. won
2. sail
3. cell
4. sell
5. one
6. sale

Unit 18
A
Bigger than:
boat
train
house
tree
man
B
Smaller than:
rabbit
mouse
fly
bee
flower
grasshopper
ball

Unit 19
A
1. cap
2. map
3. fan
4. hat
5. pan
6. tap

B
1. bad
2. sat
3. pan
4. fat

Unit 20
A
1. bed
2. net
3. ten
4. hen
5. peg
6. leg

B
1. men, ten
2. net, jet
3. get, met
4. pen, hen

Unit 21
A
1. six
2. pin
3. pig
4. lid
5. fin
6. bin

B
1. bit
2. fit
3. lit
4. sip
5. lip
6. hip

Unit 22
A
1. cot
2. mop
3. fox
4. dog
5. log
6. box

B
1. got
2. top
3. pot

4. hot
5. fog
6. hop

Unit 23
A
1. bus
2. sun
3. cup
4. tug
5. jug
6. hut
B
1. rug
2. pup
3. sun
4. tub

Unit 24
A
1. hall
2. ball
3. wall
4. small
5. fall
6. tall
B
1. try
2. dry
3. sky
4. cry
5. my
6. fly

Unit 25 Revision
A
1. bat ×
2. rug ✓
3. cat ×
4. bug ✓
5. hat ×
6. jug ✓
B
1. ten ×
2. thin ✓
3. pin ✓
4. bin ✓
5. hen ×
6. pen ×

Unit 26 Test 1
1. hat
2. hen
3. bin
4. cot
5. bun
6. ball

Unit 27 Test 2
1. pan
2. net
3. six
4. cat
5. jug
6. wall

Unit 28
1. gate
2. snail
3. fish
4. cake
5. mice
6. five
7. mask
8. clock
9. feed

Unit 29
ice:
mice
dice
eat:
seat
wheat
ate:
gate
plate

Unit 30
A
1. sky
2. live
3. table
4. baby
5. book
6. wish
B
ear:
bear
dear
fear
ace:
face
race
lace
one:
bone
done
gone

Unit 31
A
1. bell
2. nest
3. star
4. duck
5. boot
6. kite
B
1. fork
2. road
3. book

Unit 32 Revision
A
1. bird
2. four
3. hill
4. sale
5. fall
B
1. bone
2. foot
3. kite
4. cake
5. bread
6. seat

Unit 33 Test
1. rice
2. cake
3. tail
4. plate
5. fish
6. farm

Unit 34
1. blackbird
2. goldfish
3. bulldog
4. butterfly
5. football
6. waterfall

Unit 35
1. rainbow
2. pigtail
3. armchair
4. eyelash
5. starfish
6. eggcup

Unit 36
1. peg
2. bed
3. leg
4. fan

Unit 37
A
ay:
play
day
stay
hay
oy:
boy
coy
joy
toy
B
1. way
2. lay
3. tray
4. boy

Unit 38
A
1. shark
2. shell
3. ship
4. sheep
5. shoe
6. shed
B
1. shower
2. short
3. sharp
4. sheet

Unit 39
A
1. fish
2. dish
3. wash
4. bush
5. crash
6. brush
B
1. dash
2. rash
3. wish
4. ash

Unit 40
1. clock
2. lock
3. sack
4. sock
5. duck
6. chick
B
1. lick
2. black
3. rock
4. kick

Unit 41
A
1. chair
2. cheese
3. chin
4. peach
5. beach
6. chain
B
1. branch
2. child
3. cherry
4. chat

Unit 42
A
1. broom
2. spoon
3. roof
4. root
5. moon
6. boot

Unit 43 Revision
ck:
clock
duck
sh:
fish
ship
ch:

chain
chair

Unit 44 Test 1
1. ship
2. hay
3. crash
4. lock
5. chair
6. moon

Unit 45 Test 2
1. coy
2. shoe
3. crush
4. sock
5. chair
6. boot

Unit 46
1. mop
2. lip
3. cup
4. bat
5. peg
6. bed
7. bus
8. cow
9. pin
10. nut
11. sun
12. hat
13. gun
14. pot
15. boy

Unit 47
1. fish
2. hand
3. back
4. crust
5. bell
6. doll
7. truck
8. lock
9. five
10. bone
11. plug
12. wave
13. nest
14. neck
15. crab
16. ship
17. brush
18. tent

Unit 48
1. map
2. ant
3. pen
4. ship
5. flower
6. pig
7. egg
8. fan
9. duck
10. nest
11. net
12. log
13. ice
14. pond
15. milk

Unit 49
1. peg
2. gun
3. cup
4. tap
5. broom
6. crab
7. sit
8. bed
9. fox
10. map
11. clock
12. frog
13. rug
14. bug
15. pan
16. cow
17. fly
18. spoon

Unit 50 Revision
1. drum O
2. frog ✓
3. arm O
4. flag ✓
5. bib ×
6. crab ×

Unit 51 Test
1. bed
2. crab
3. back
4. ship
5. spoon
6. frog

Unit 52
1. arm
2. ant
3. pea
4. cat
5. dog
6. tea

Unit 53
1. tap
2. owl
3. net
4. bus
5. pin
6. rat

Unit 54
A
1. bus
2. bat
3. bird
4. box
5. boy
6. ball

B
1. cap
2. cat
3. car
4. cot
5. cow
6. cake

Unit 55
A
1. arm
2. jar
3. dart
4. star
5. card
6. car

B
1. dark
2. bark
3. farm
4. park
5. are

Unit 56
A
1. horse
2. torch
3. story
4. fork
5. corn
6. storm

B
1. short
2. sports
3. sore
4. corner

Unit 57
A
1. boat
2. coat
3. goat
4. loaf
5. road
6. soap

B
1. toad
2. load
3. oats
4. coach
5. coast
6. soak
7. float
8. toad
9. croak

Unit 58
A
1. chain
2. train
3. tail
4. nail
5. snail
6. sail

B
1. maid
2. mail
3. rain
4. drain
5. hail
6. paint

Unit 59
A
1. bee
2. peel
3. three
4. seed
5. tree
6. teeth

B
1. sleep
2. week
3. street
4. meet
5. seen
6. green

Unit 60
A
1. flag
2. brush
3. drum
4. cloud
5. crab
6. frog

B
1. nest
2. ant
3. lamp
4. hand
5. belt
6. milk

Unit 61 Revision
ar:
car
star
jar
dart
or:
corn
horse
story
horn
oa:
soap
loaf
boat
road

Unit 62 Test 1
1. star
2. fork

3. goat
4. snail
5. three
6. crab

Unit 63 Test 2
1. coat
2. tail
3. peel
4. crab
5. story
6. car

Unit 64
1. nest
2. cone
3. clock
4. flag
5. bear
6. moon
7. mouse
8. bell
9. boat
10. ring
11. nine
12. cave

Unit 65
1. chip
2. shell
3. glove
4. mice
5. frog
6. wing
7. seat
8. seal
9. sheep
10. house
11. swing
12. fast

Unit 66
1. bag
2. ship
3. rain
4. duck
5. crab
6. gate

Unit 67
1. shell
2. window
3. brick
4. finger
5. chicken
6. house
7. garden
8. rabbit
9. donkey
10. plant

Unit 68 Revision

A
1. snow
2. milk
3. coat
4. star
5. drum
6. house

B
1. truck
2. ship
3. spoon
4. crown

Unit 69 Test
1. snow
2. shell
3. house
4. boat
5. clock
6. wave

Unit 70
1. bed
2. yellow
3. brown
4. black
5. green
6. blue

Unit 71
1. gun
2. six
3. mat
4. mop
5. pig
6. sun

Unit 72

A
1. dog
2. dish
3. doll
4. door
5. duck
6. drum

B
1. tail
2. tree
3. toy
4. tap
5. tent
6. toe

Unit 73 Review

A

oy:
toy
boy

all:
wall
call

ay:
play
stay

B
1. duck
2. deer
3. book
4. crab
5. shoe
6. truck

Unit 74 Test 1
1. bin
2. map
3. ball
4. fin
5. toy
6. ship

Unit 75 Test 2
1. sheep
2. roof
3. chair
4. sick
5. rash
6. star

Unit 76 Test 3
1. book
2. milk
3. drum
4. flag
5. coat
6. corn